KAFFE FASSETT'S
quilts in the sun

featuring Roberta Horton • Mary Mashuta • Liza Prior Lucy • Pauline Smith • Brandon Mably • Rebekah Lynch • Betsy Menefee Rickles

A ROWAN BOOK

The Taunton Press

Big Star Quilt

The Taunton Press
Inspiration for hands-on living®

The Taunton Press
63 South Main St. PO Box 5506
Newtown, CT 06470-5506
www.taunton.com
10 9 8 7 6 5 4 3

First Published in Great Britain in 2007 by Rowan Yarns
Copyright © Rowan Yarns 2007

Art Director: Kaffe Fassett
Technical editors: Ruth Eglinton and Pauline Smith
Co-ordinator: Pauline Smith
Publishing Consultant: Susan Berry
Patchwork Designs: Kaffe Fassett, Roberta Horton,
                       Rebekah Lynch, Mary Mashuta,
                       Liza Prior Lucy, Betsy Menefee Rickles,
                       Pauline Smith, Brandon Mably.

Quilters: Judy Irish, Pauline Smith
Sewers for Liza Prior Lucy quilts: Judy Baldwin,
                                    Corienne Kramer

Photography: Debbie Patterson
Flat shot photography: Dave Tolson @ Visage

Styling: Kaffe Fassett
Design Layout: Christine Wood - Gallery of Quilts/
                                       cover/front section
                       Simon Wagstaff - instructions &
                                        technical information

Illustrations: Ruth Eglinton
Feature: Amy Butler

Library of Congress Cataloging-in-Publication Data

Fassett, Kaffe.
Patchwork and quilting book. Number 9 : Kaffe Fassett's quilts
in the sun : 20 designs from Rowan for Patchwork and Quilting
: featuring Roberta Horton, Brandon Mably, Rebekah Lynch,
Betsy Menefee Rickles.
p. cm.
ISBN 978-1-56158-991-3
1. Patchwork--Patterns. 2. Quilting--Patterns. 3. Quilts. I. Title.
II. Title: Quilts in the sun.

TT835.F369 2007
746.46'041--dc22
2007020490

Colour reproduction by Chroma Graphics (Overseas) Pte. Ltd
Printed and bound in Singapore by KHL. Printing Co. Pte. Ltd

contents

introduction

As I look over this year's crop of new quilts I see two themes emerging. The first is the use of triangles. Six quilts and a cushion use this basic shape in wonderfully contrasting ways. My *Lady of the Lake* is after an old American quilt I have been drawn to for years: it uses large and small triangles in contrast to create a deliciously alive revelation. I enjoyed using my earthy browns and golds against cream – an unusual Autumn toned palette for me.

Frothy, for which Liza and I have both done versions, was in our book, *Glorious Patchwork*. The layout is simple squares sliced in half to create pleasing contrasts. Many old English and Dutch quilts use this formation. It comes from a period in my patchwork designing when flowery furnishing prints really appealed to me. Because I was so smitten with blowsy florals I started designing them myself and commissioned Philip Jacobs (the king of English chintz) to do some lush florals for us. I love feeding new colour schemes into his wonderful old documents which he paints so expressively.

In Liza's *Tropical Frothy* she uses all Amy Butler prints to celebrate Amy joining our team at Rowan. In my blue and white version I use my new florals plus Philip's new line. But I found using some of Amy's more graphic designs was a perfect foil for the painterly realism of Philip and me. I used Amy's prints in a similar way in *Framed Jar*. This is my attempt at a mainly blue and white theme to go with the tiles I knew we would find on our Portuguese shoot. The border triangles in different scales appealed to me and I have always been attracted to the pennant-like points in the last border. Mary Mashuta's *Goes Around Comes Around* has a delicious movement, it puts me in mind of a Snakes and Ladders board with the swirls in my Paisley Jungle fabric.

OPPOSITE: *Framed Jar Quilt*
BELOW RIGHT: *Goes Around Comes Around Quilt*
BELOW CENTRE: *Tropical Frothy Quilt*
BELOW: *Lady of the Lake Quilt*

The other theme in my contributed designs is the idea of framing colour and prints with sashing or borders. *Jane's Diamonds* is after the famous Jane Austen quilt – I've done only the centre. What thrilled me about this concept was the isolating of 'fussy cut' mirror image prints. They look so jewel-like and fresh on their cream or deep blue sashing.

Earthy Frames and *Sunny Frames* isolate the centres of blocks even further with quite heavy borders in each. I was intrigued to see how reversing the borders, prints inside dark shot cotton frames in *Earthy*, then pastel prints framing blocks of bright plain colour in *Sunny* changed the look of the quilt dramatically. My floral stripe cushion combines both these themes. It is done in triangles, but the pattern creates square frames that look to me like Russian ribbons.

Floral Parade really frames the flowery prints that dominate our new collection – I couldn't resist doing a full-blown pastel number using Amy Butler's joyful Polka-dot for many of the borders. Changing mood completely to do a deep brown/red story, Chartreuse shot cotton works a treat for the frames.

In Roberta's *Brick Bracket Medallion* quilt Amy Butler's Royal Garden fabric with peacocks and palaces is cleverly framed by a series of pieced and striped borders.

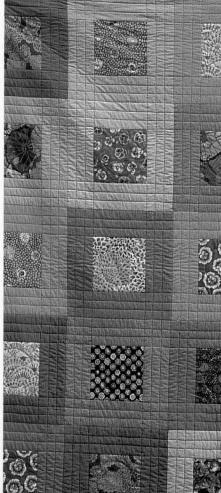

ABOVE: *Red Floral Parade Quilt*
ABOVE RIGHT: *Pastel Floral Parade Quilt*
RIGHT: *Brick Bracket Medallion Quilt detail showing Royal Garden fabric.*

OPPOSITE TOP: *Jane's Diamonds Pastel Quilt*
OPPOSITE FAR LEFT: *Jane's Diamonds Lapis Quilt*
OPPOSITE CENTRE: *Earthy Frames Quilt*
LEFT: *Sunny Frames Quilt*

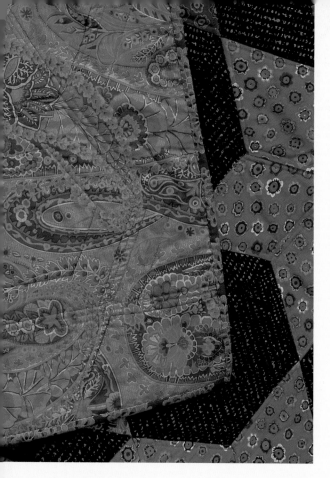

the fabrics

Paisley Jungle

When I first got to London the elegant old store of Liberty's had a collection of Paisley fabrics on sale that took my breath away. They were so large scale and detailed in magnificent colourways. I have been collecting books on Paisley ever since and finally I've done my first large-scale version with small flowers and geranium leaves, which I love because they have such definite markings. I am passionate about the deep jewel tones but best of all the soft pastel and yellow versions remind me of antique faded Paisley you might find in the antique markets of Europe.

Paper Fans

As a child I always loved making paper fans. When I got to Japan as a grown-up artist, I saw so many beautiful fans. Real ones with glorious painted motifs and stylized layers of fans on fabric and pottery. I tried my own version after making striped fans for a huge Christmas tree for the Victoria & Albert Museum in London.

Samarkand

I love quilts that contain circular motifs and dotted fabrics. I like to design as many fabrics as I can with spots and dots so I can combine them in my quilts. When I'd finished painting out this pattern I felt it looked like metal studs on old leather riding gear or like primitive jewelry. I like how delicate it can look in soft pastel yet how masculine and strong it is in deep dark colours.

Floating Flowers

I have a beautiful porcelain box in my bathroom that I bought in a china shop in London. The stylized round flowers used to stare at me as I bathed, begging to be used in a design. Finally after several years I produced this print. Thank you, box!

Verbena

I bought a small book on flowers depicted in delicate watercolor and Verbenas jumped out at me as I thumbed through it. The delicious variety of soft pastels on these little clusters of blooms seemed just right for a fabric; it could work well as a long border, the straight stems becoming a stripe, or just as a fluffy mass of color when cutting smaller pieces.

Minton

Every now and then I treat myself to a really juicy bit of china from one of the many antique porcelain collections available in London. A fabulous Minton jug smothered in flowers (just the kind I'm always looking for) inspired this fabric. I love how it becomes a laid-back brocade in some contexts and a lively floral in others.

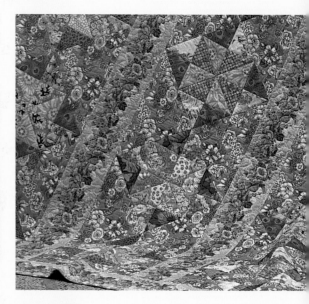

Potentilla

Firstly I love the flowers of the Potentilla plant – they are small poppy-like blooms with a dark spot on each petal. The lay out for this print I lifted from a china tea set I have with roses surrounded by leaves. The pastel colours bring a good light element to a quilt while the deeper reds and greens add a rich color note. See *left*.

Floral Stripes

When I was doing one of my favourite walks through Paris, which never fails to fill me with inspiration, I spotted an Empire period enamelled egg with tumbling roses on a sky blue stripe. It zapped into my memory and I rushed home to design.

I could see this fabric being used with many other stripes in a version of Handkerchief Corners or Mitred Boxes, like the cushion I've done.

Philip Jacobs' New Collection

From Philip's extensive archive of old French and English documents we found the lively Geranium, the old-fashioned Foxglove, the blowsy Luscious (Peonies and Plums) and Morning Glories. The Hollyhocks on brocade creates a beautiful stripe which also reads as an all-over floral, and the Coral Leaf is a dynamic classic that I've used as a border in *Frothy* and on the jar in *Framed Jar*. See *opposite top left and opposite bottom right*.

Tropical Frothy by Liza Prior Lucy
The limes, oranges and blues of Liza's *Tropical Frothy* make a fresh contrast with the blue and white tiled mural.

13

Jane's Diamonds Pastel by Kaffe Fassett
I love the way the lattice glass door mirrors
the diamonds in my quilt. The morning light
enhances the quilt.

15

Lady of the Lake
by Kaffe Fassett
The simple geometry of
my quilt is echoed in the
structure of this
staircase.

Gilded Snowballs by Kaffe Fassett
The late afternoon sunshine lights
up my *Gilded Snowballs*.

Earthy Frames by Kaffe Fassett
This peeling brown door is just the perfect colour to show off my *Earthy Frames*.

Sunny Frames by Kaffe Fassett
I love the way the tiled border picks up the golden colours of *Sunny Frames*.

Delft Star by Kaffe Fassett
I just had to use this magnificent blue tiled church wall. The only way I could was
to stretch the quilt across my back.

Jane's Diamonds Lapis
by Kaffe Fassett
Against this mossy
garden wall *Jane's
Diamonds Lapis* has a
luminous quality.

Chelsea by Pauline Smith
Pauline's *Chelsea* looking quite at home wrapped around a wrought iron gate.

Octagons with Stars by Pauline Smith
Pauline designed her quilt with the blue and white tiles of Portugal in mind.

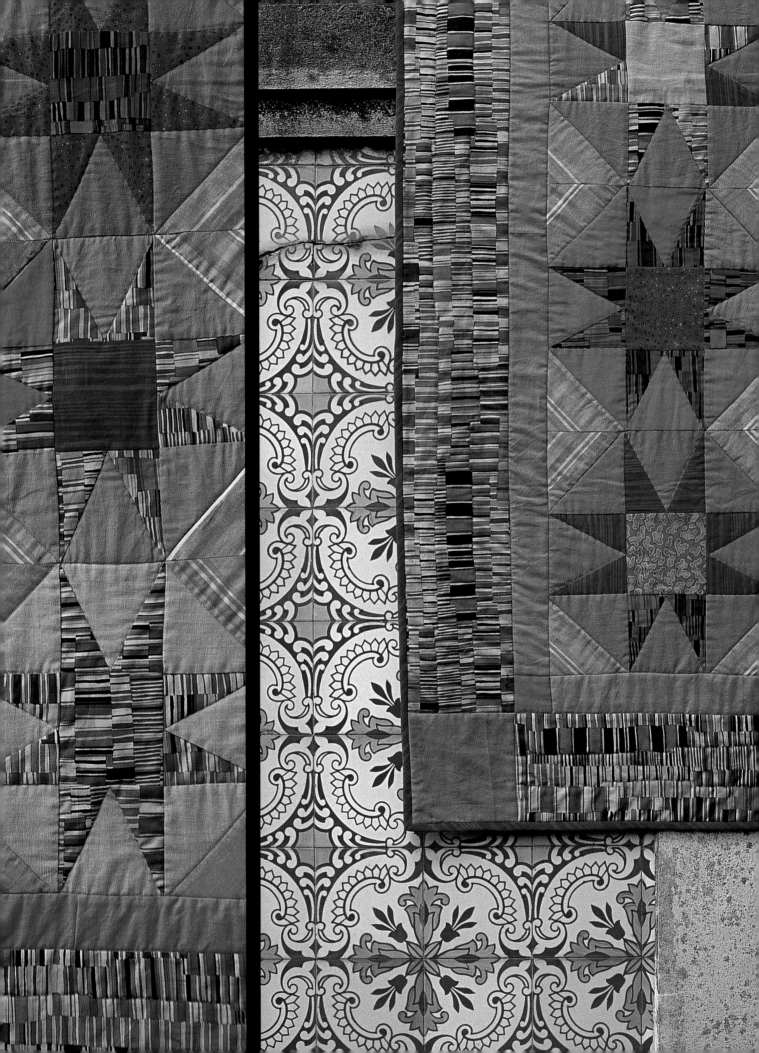

Forget Me Not Cabins by Betsy Menefee Rickles
We were so lucky to find this market stall with yellow buckets of flowers for
Betsy's *Forget Me Not Cabins*.

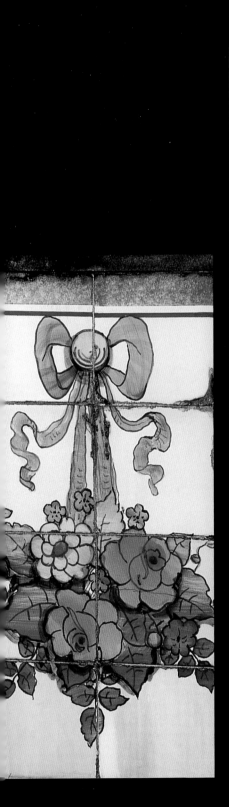

Brick Bracket Medallion
by Roberta Horton
Roberta's *Brick Bracket Medallion* looks great against the tiled wall and wrought iron furniture.

Framed Jar by Kaffe Fassett
I had to plead with the owner of this tile shop for permission to hang my *Framed Jar* from his balcony. I think it was worth it. The detail shot shows the jar in Coral Leaf fabric against my Potentilla fabric and the border of blue Minton.

Blue Portugal by Liza Prior Lucy

Red Floral Parade by Kaffe Fassett
My *Red Floral Parade* showcasing Philip's floral prints.
I'm pleased with how my Jungle Paisley in rust looks
as the quilt backing, shown at the entrance of York
House Hotel, Lisbon.

Pastel Floral Parade by Kaffe Fassett
The delicate pink walls of the church perfectly match the pastels in my quilt. The detail shows

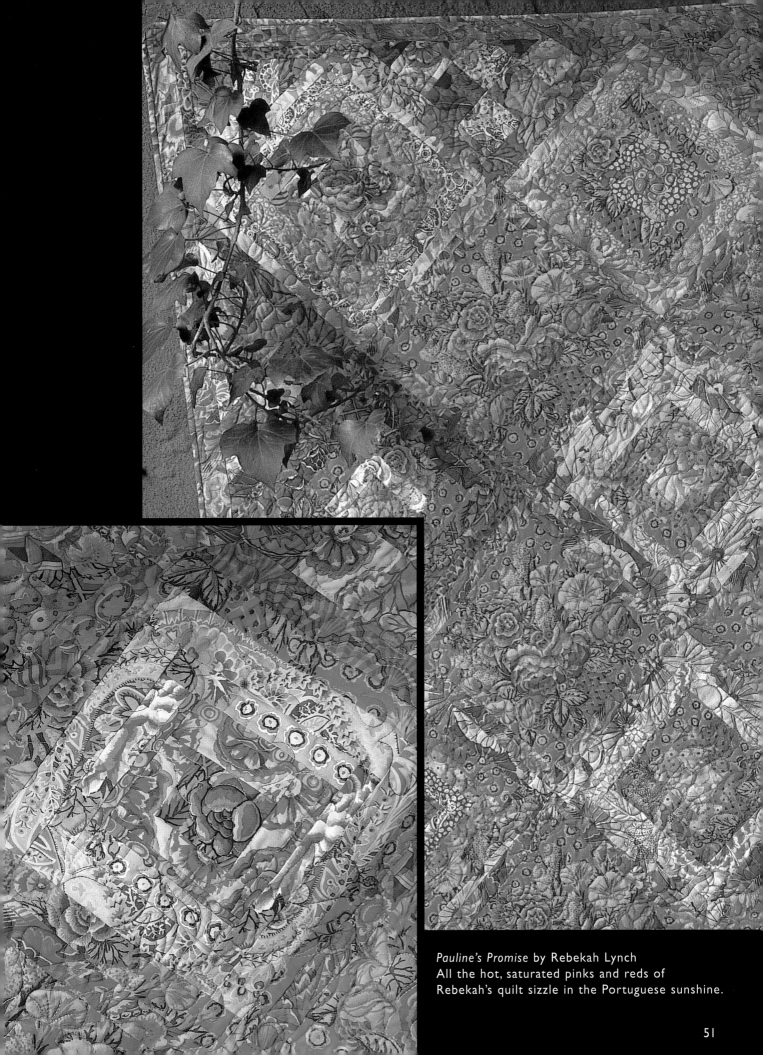

Pauline's Promise by Rebekah Lynch
All the hot, saturated pinks and reds of
Rebekah's quilt sizzle in the Portuguese sunshine.

Blue and White Frothy by Kaffe Fassett

Blue And White Frothy, using my large florals with those of Philip and Amy is bordered with

amy butler's midwest modern

Everyday I reflect on how fortunate I am to be doing this creative work that I love so much. I realized I wanted to become an artist as soon as I learned what the word artist meant as a young girl. I was always coloring and crafting and making homemade gifts for friends and family. I excelled at drawing mushrooms, frogs, and flowers. It was, after all, the 70's. This might be the caveat to my style. If my work feels groovy at times, it's because I allow myself to think the way I did as a little girl—with curiosity and excitement. If anything, I'm less hindered now, because as a child I tied myself to the icons of the times. I felt the same kindred love of nature that was driving the styles of the era.

My mom and grandmother, both self-taught artists, are a huge influence on me. When I was little, I watched both of them dabble and often master every craft. They created water color paintings, hooked rugs, knitted, quilted, and made dioramas with found antique artefacts and dried flowers, truly making our home a creative nest. My grandmother gave me my first fabric stash and would always keep me supplied with craft materials. I took that first sack of fabric and glued together halter tops for my little friends in my neighborhood because I didn't have a sewing machine at home. It was all about the fabric and the giving. My friends tried to wear the outfits and assured me it was *the thought that counts*—a comment I still often get as I love to experiment on my friends with new ideas.

Later in art school I became obsessed with surface design and fashion. I would draw enormously tall women with impossible necks and on them I would create lavish, layered clothing. Within those layers, I would draw in florals, patterns, stripes, and modern geometric shapes. I found that the passionate creation of the print outweighed my love of the clothing. *And*, they wouldn't let me glue together halter tops in art school, so I focused my efforts on the design of pattern.

In art school I met my future husband David. We formed a unique bond that continues to this day. We have great mutual respect for each other as artists and as people. Twenty years into our relationship,

we still work very well together and remain joined-at-the-hip. We've had an amazing and diverse career already, moving from illustration to retail design, to developing books and becoming contributing editors for magazines. All the while, we continued our explorations and exhibits of fine art. When we started our studio, we didn't feel we needed to move to either coast, but felt we needed to move home to be near our families. With blind enthusiasm we moved, quit our jobs, and launched Art of the Midwest. We soon realized that our choices, however fiscally difficult, would be paid forward with amazing opportunities and creative freedom. The hilly rural farm country of Ohio became our fertile field of dreams. Fifteen years later, and after a few more moves, we've landed in Granville surrounded by our friends and family, still making a go of it, and still finding our work fulfilling and exciting.

The two of us share other passions as well, paramount being the love of outdoors. The inspiration of the garden is pretty obvious in my work. Gardening is seasonal, just like fabrics. And like designing, it relies on learning, studying, and creativity. The challenges of a Midwestern climate, conditions, physics, scale, timing, water, fungus, etc. simply don't exist in the safety of my studio. The worst that might happen in design is I spill some tea on a print or one of the cats chews a corner. Gardening creates kinetic art through combinations and textures. It's really about the collection, and how it all works together with scale, color, texture, time, and all the other elements that make a garden grow.

Several of my close friends have the same passion. So like every other creative aspect of my life, we share ideas and materials. Plant swaps are common, as are seasonal runs to particular greenhouses in surrounding areas and neighboring states. Frankly, in springtime it's somewhat hard for me to focus on designing indoors when I'm daydreaming of amended soil, hellebores, banana trees, boxwood and hydrangeas. David and I have created a tropical mood that suites our California modern house style. It feels surprising yet familiar here in the hills of Ohio, and it inspires me to keep thinking outside my comfort zone—or at least our climate zone.

The inspiration of nature as a whole, flora and fauna, is my constant. The natural world has always been a big influence. I grew up with an appreciation for wildlife and flowers. Our home was always filled with animals and my mother taught me about wildflowers and birds. My grandmother was a prolific gardener, and I have many memories of spending long summer days in her yard helping her tend to her flowers and vegetables.

My home life and my surroundings also play a big part in what inspires me. Mine and David's various collections of antiques and curiosities over the years have greatly affected my design voice. Like most things, they change depending on where I am in my life. My home is a reflection of where I am creatively, just like the fabrics. The collections in my studio space are also very personal. I'm surrounded by all the things I love: loads of material, notions, antiques, ephemera and books. My obsession with antique fabrics, and a collection that's been growing 20 years now, has influenced my design eye and passion for unique vintage prints.

Broadly, all decorative arts and textiles have greatly influenced my work. This of course includes fashion. I've gone through several love affairs with different genres and periods of design. Culturally I'm hugely inspired by ethnic textiles and artifacts and I would collect more if I had the space! I have very eclectic tastes and I am influenced by every era, from turn of the century to mid-century. To me, design is far more interesting and fun when you experiment with many different elements.

The luxury of my surroundings is quite simple. An unfettered lifestyle that allows me to focus on the creative work that I want to do without the stress or influences of a larger city. Don't get me wrong, I *love* the cities and visit them all when I can, especially New York. But it's spoiling to visit on a cultural junket and then go back to my small town and edit my inspiration in the comfort of my peaceful surroundings. I take that easy and approachable voice, and let it live in my work, which evokes my

modern sensibilities. Ergo: Midwest Modern. I design what I love, and what I want to be surrounded with. I'm always dreaming of future fabrics I could sew with or use in my home which is always the underlying motivation for specific prints. I keep things fresh and lively by keeping my inspiration kinetic. Dave and I call our home/studio the "design lab" because we are always test-driving my new fabrics all around the house in the forms of slipcovers, pillows and clothing. I'm always excited about a new "color" or colors. I keep an on-going color idea stash where I save snips of colors I love which eventually get worked into my palettes. My goal is to enjoy the entire creative process while I'm designing. I feel this joy and energy is translated in my work and hopefully passes onto others. I'm fortunate that folks respond sincerely to what I do which is incredibly humbling and gives me the greatest pleasure! I'm so enthusiastic to work with Rowan because they nurture the artist and allow for the most natural transitions from creation to production. It's beyond wonderful really. My Belle and Lotus collections happened so organically. They allow me to create in my most comfortable fashion, and we build on each other's enthusiasm and ideas. I'm excited to launch a brand new home decor collection with Rowan called Nigella. I'm describing this group as having a neo-Victorian vibe, with a mixture of modern elements and feminine details: it's very romantic and rich looking. I am working through the first strike-offs now and soon we'll have advance yardage to sew up samples for photography and the quilt market. My new sewing book, *In Stitches,* has been doing very well and it's inspired me to create four new patterns for spring, two are fashion driven and two are for home dec projects. It's a non-stop whirlwind of creation, and I'm so thankful I have a great group of seamstresses in my community to help test and produce our new projects. It's never a dull moment and that's we all love about working together!

Most important in my world is the company I keep. My friends, family, work mates and pets. They are the reason I enjoy my studio and my life as an artist.

To see more of Amy's work, visit www.amybutlerdesign.com

Lady of the Lake Quilt ★★

Kaffe Fassett

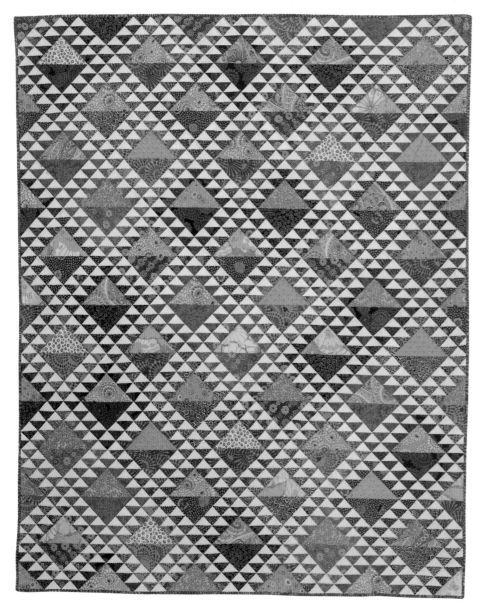

This old layout has haunted me until I finally designed one. The contrasting clarity created by cream and deep autumn tones is rare for me but I like the effect.

SIZE OF QUILT
The finished quilt will measure approx. 70¾in x 85in (179.75cm x 216cm).

MATERIALS
Patchwork Fabrics:
ROOTLETS
Burnt Orange   CM07BO: ⅝yd (60cm)
Mauve   CM07MV: ¼yd (25cm)
STARSHINE
Mauve   CM08MV: ¼yd (25cm)
ROMAN GLASS
Gold   GP01GD: ¼yd (25cm)

LOTUS LEAF
Yellow   GP29YE: ¼yd (25cm)
ORGANIC DOTS
Brown   GP53BR: ⅝yd (60cm)
Contrast   GP53CO: ¼yd (25cm)
Gold   GP53GD: ⅝yd (60cm)
FLOATING FLOWERS
Brown   GP56BR: ¾yd (70cm)
Yellow   GP56YE: ⅜yd (35cm)
PAPER FANS
Brown   GP57BR: ¾yd (70cm)
Ochre   GP57OC: ⅝yd (60cm)

SAMARKAND
Ochre   GP58OC: ⅝yd (60cm)
Stone   GP58ST: ½yd (45cm)
GUINEA FLOWER
Brown   GP59BR: ¾yd (70cm)
PAISLEY JUNGLE
Tangerine   GP60TN: ¼yd (25cm)
SHOT COTTON
Blush   SC28: 3¼yds (3m)

Backing Fabric: 5¼yds (4.8m)
We suggest these fabrics for backing:

SHAGGY POPPY Mustard, PJ03MU
FLOATING FLOWERS Yellow, GP56YE

Binding:
PAPER FANS
Brown   GP57BR: ⅝yd (60cm)

Batting:
78in × 93in (198cm × 236cm).

Quilting thread:
Dark brown hand quilting thread.

Templates:

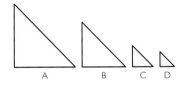

A   B   C   D

PATCH SHAPES
This traditional Lady of the Lake block which finishes to 10in (25.5cm) is made using 2 triangle patch shapes (Templates A and C). The blocks are set 'on point' and stitched into diagonal rows, the edges and corners of the quilt are filled in using half and quarter blocks. These use the 2 main triangle shapes and 2 additional triangle patch shapes (Templates B and D).

CUTTING OUT
Cut the fabric in the order stated.
Template A: Cut 6⅞in (17.5cm) strips across the width of the fabric. Each strip will give you 12 patches per 45in (114cm) wide fabric. Cut 6⅞in (17.5cm) squares, then cut each square once diagonally to make 2 triangles, using the template as a guide. Cut 12 in GP56YE, 10 in GP60TN, 8 in CM07MV, GP29YE, 7 in GP57BR, 6 in CM07BO, CM08MV, GP53BR, GP53GD, GP56BR, GP57OC, GP58OC, GP59BR, 5 in GP01GD, GP53CO and GP58ST. Reserve leftover strips and trim for template B.
Template B: Using the leftover strips from template A, trim to 5⅛in (13cm). Cut 5⅛in (13cm) squares, then cut each square once diagonally to make 2 triangles, using the template as a guide. Cut 5 in GP01GD, 3 in GP29YE, 2 in CM07MV, GP53BR, GP56BR, GP56YE, GP57BR, GP57OC, GP58OC and GP59BR.
Template C: Cut 2⅞in (7.25cm) strips across the width of the fabric. Each strip will give you 28 patches per 45in (114cm) wide fabric. Cut 2⅞in (7.25cm) squares, then cut each square once diagonally to make 2

triangles, using the template as a guide. Cut 948 in SC28, 133 in GP57BR, 117 in GP56BR, 113 in GP59BR, 106 in GP53BR, 104 in GP58OC, 103 in GP57OC, 96 in CM07BO, GP53GD and 80 in GP58ST. Reserve leftover strips and trim for template D.
Template D: Using the leftover strips from template C, trim to 2¼in (5.75cm). Cut 2¼in (5.75cm) squares, then cut each square once diagonally to make 2 triangles, using the template as a guide. Cut 24 in SC28, 5 in GP53BR, GP59BR, 4 in GP56BR, GP57BR, GP57OC and 2 in GP58OC.

Binding: Cut 8 strips 2½in (6.5cm) wide × width of fabric in GP57BR.

Backing: Cut 1 piece 44in × 93in (112cm ×

236cm) and 1 piece 35in × 93in (89cm × 236cm) in backing fabric.

MAKING THE BLOCKS
Use a ¼in (6mm) seam allowance throughout. Referring to the quilt assembly diagram for fabric placement piece 50 blocks as shown in the block assembly diagrams a and b. The finished full block, turned 'on point' can be seen in diagram c. The top and bottom of the quilt are filled in by piecing horizontal half blocks, pieced in the same way as the main blocks. Take care that the pale SC28 background triangles are in the correct positions. The sides of the quilt are filled in by making vertical half blocks, as shown in diagram d. These use the additional 2 template shapes B and D. The blocks are

Block Assembly Diagrams

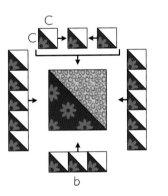

a

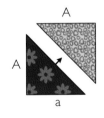

b

c

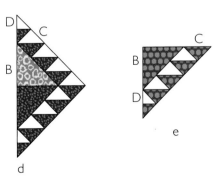

d

e

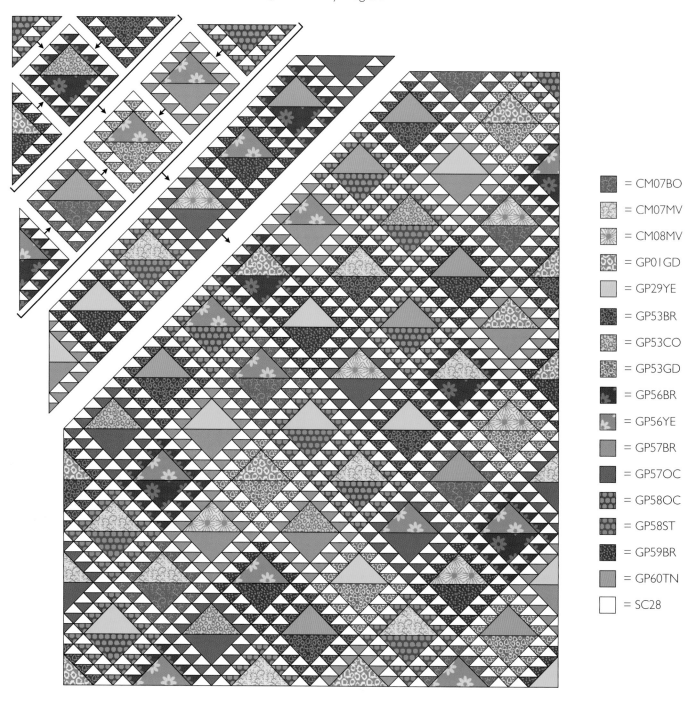

▦	= CM07BO
▦	= CM07MV
▦	= CM08MV
▦	= GP01GD
▦	= GP29YE
▦	= GP53BR
▦	= GP53CO
▦	= GP53GD
▦	= GP56BR
▦	= GP56YE
▦	= GP57BR
▦	= GP57OC
▦	= GP58OC
▦	= GP58ST
▦	= GP59BR
▦	= GP60TN
☐	= SC28

reversed on the opposite side of the quilt. The quilt corners are completed by piecing 4 quarter blocks, (see diagram e) each is different so refer to the quilt assembly diagram for guidance.

MAKING THE QUILT
Lay out all the full blocks in diagonal rows,

then fill in the edges and corners with the half and quarter blocks as shown in the quilt assembly diagram. Carefully separate into diagonal rows and join. Join the rows to form the quilt.

FINISHING THE QUILT
Press the quilt top. Seam the backing pieces

using a ¼in (6mm) seam allowance to form a piece approx. 78in x 93in (198cm x 236cm). Layer the quilt top, batting and backing and baste together (see page 139). Using dark brown hand quilting thread, quilt in the ditch along all the seam lines. Trim the quilt edges and attach the binding (see page 140).

Earthy Frames Quilt ★

KAFFE FASSETT

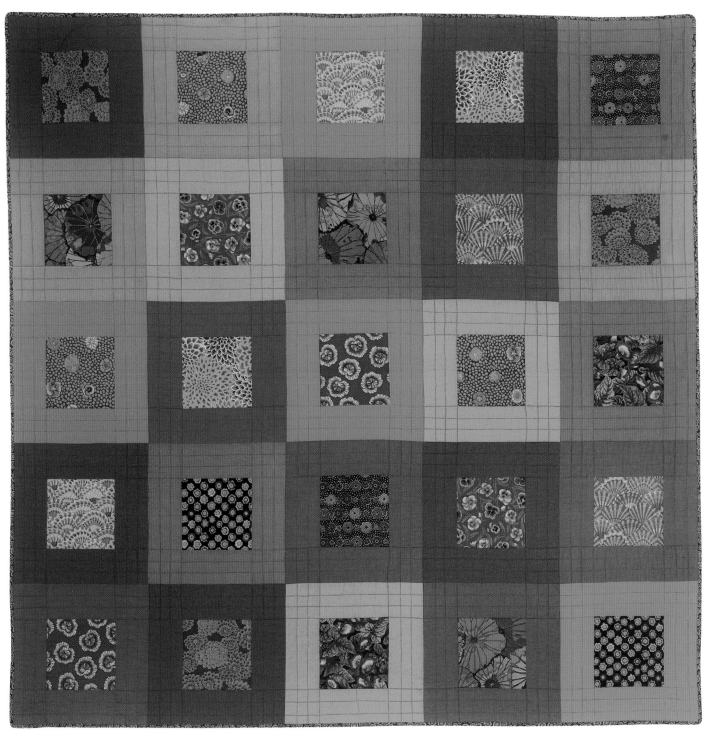

The deep glow of these close shades of bronzy browns make this quilt work in antique wood panelled rooms or very contemporary graphic spaces. The simple quilting emphasizes the geometric strength of this design.

SIZE OF QUILT

The finished quilt will measure approx. 75in x 75in (190.5cm x 190.5cm).

MATERIALS

Patchwork Fabrics:

LOTUS LEAF
Umber   GP29UM: ¼yd (25cm)
AURICULA
Black   GP52BK: ¼yd (25cm)
DAHLIA BLOOMS
Autumn   GP54AT: ¼yd (25cm)
FLOATING FLOWERS
Brown   GP56BR: ¼yd (25cm)
PAPER FANS
Brown   GP57BR: ¼yd (25cm)
Ochre   GP57OC: ¼yd (25cm)
SAMARKAND
Charcoal   GP58CC: ¼yd (25cm)
GUINEA FLOWER
Brown   GP59BR: ¼yd (25cm)
PANSY
Oxblood   PJ01OX: ¼yd (25cm)
TRUMPET FLOWER
Black   PJ02BK: ¼yd (25cm)
GERANIUM LEAF
Sludge   PJ05SL: ¼yd (25cm)
SHOT COTTON
Moor   SC52: ⅞yd (80cm)
Nut   SC53: 1⅛yds (1m)
Brick   SC58: ¾ yd (70cm)
Caramel   SC59: ⅝yd (60cm)
Clay   SC60: ⅝yd (60cm)
Terracotta   SC61: ¾ yd (70cm)

Backing Fabric:
The backing for this quilt was pieced from 2 Shot Cotton fabrics, SC53 and SC61, however any of the Shot Cottons used in the quilt would be suitable.
For 2 fabrics use 2⅜yds (2.15m) of each, or alternatively 4¾yds (4.35m) of any one of the fabrics.

Binding:
ORGANIC DOTS
Brown   GP53BR: ⅝yd (60cm)

Batting:
83in x 83in (211cm x 211cm).

Quilting thread:
Dark brown machine quilting thread.

Templates:

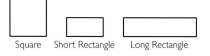

Square   Short Rectangle   Long Rectangle

PATCH SHAPES

Simple square blocks which finish to 15in (38cm) are made using 1 square patch shape (Square) and 2 rectangle patch shapes (Long and Short Rectangle). All are cut to size and no templates are provided for these very simple shapes.

CUTTING OUT

Cut the fabric in the order stated.

Squares: Cut 8in (20.25cm) squares. Cut 3 in GP29UM, GP56BR, GP59BR, 2 in GP52BK, GP54AT, GP57BR, GP57OC, GP58CC, PJ01OX, PJ02BK and PJ05SL.

Long Rectangles: Cut 4¼in (10.75cm) strips across the width of the fabric. Cut 4¼in x 15½in (10.75cm x 39.5cm) rectangles. Cut 12 in SC53, 10 in SC52, 8 in SC58, SC61, 6 in SC59 and SC60. Reserve the left over strips for the Short Rectangles.

Short Rectangles: Cut 4¼in (10.75cm) strips across the width of the fabric. Cut 4¼in x 8in (10.75cm x 20.25cm) rectangles. Also use the leftovers from the Long Rectangles. Cut 12 in SC53, 10 in SC52, 8 in SC58, SC61, 6 in SC59 and SC60.

Binding: Cut 8 strips 2½in (6.5cm) wide x width of fabric in GP53BR.

Backing: Cut 2 pieces 44in x 83in (112cm x 211cm) in backing fabric.

MAKING THE BLOCKS

Use a ¼in (6mm) seam allowance throughout. Referring to the quilt assembly diagram for fabric placement piece 25 blocks as shown in the block assembly diagram. Note that the position of the long and short rectangles alternates across the whole quilt. Pay particular attention to the blocks with Paper Fans fabric in the centres, make sure the fans will be the right way up when placed in their final position with the rectangles in the correct orientation.

MAKING THE QUILT

Join the blocks into 5 rows of 5 blocks as shown in the quilt assembly diagram. Join the rows to form the quilt.

FINISHING THE QUILT

Press the quilt top. Seam the backing pieces using a ¼in (6mm) seam allowance to form a piece approx. 83in x 83in (211cm x 211cm). Layer the quilt top, batting and backing and baste together (see page 139). Using dark brown machine quilting thread, quilt in the ditch around the centre squares and in the block seams, then 2 parallel lines in the shot cotton sections, spaced at 1¼in and 2½in (3.25cm and 6.25cm) from the block centres. Trim the quilt edges and attach the binding (see page 140).

Block Assembly Diagram

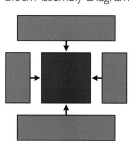

Quilt Assembly Diagram

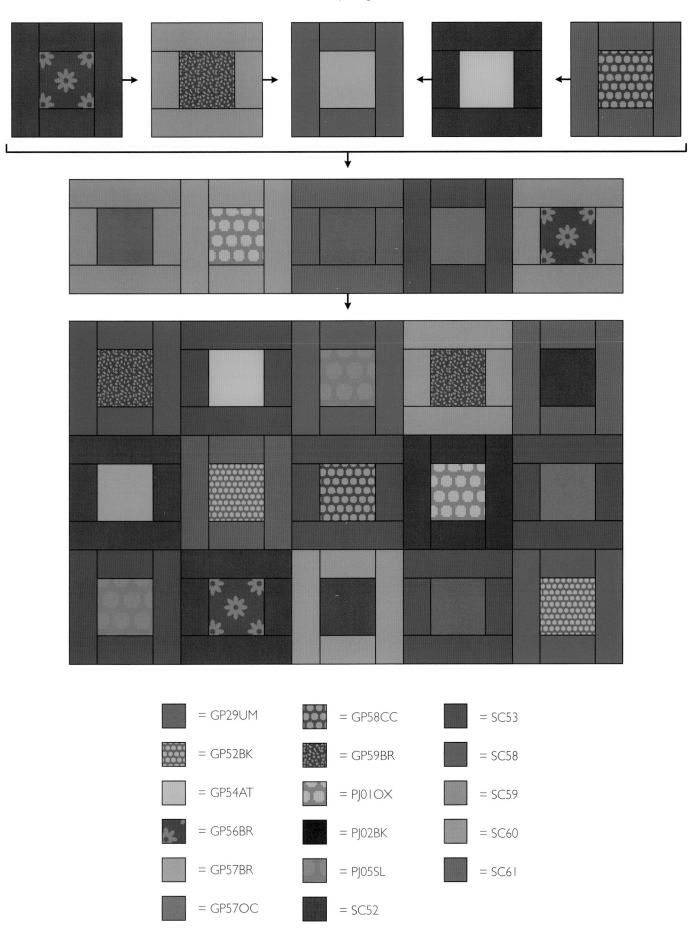

= GP29UM

= GP52BK

= GP54AT

= GP56BR

= GP57BR

= GP57OC

= GP58CC

= GP59BR

= PJ01OX

= PJ02BK

= PJ05SL

= SC52

= SC53

= SC58

= SC59

= SC60

= SC61

Sunny Frames Quilt ★

Kaffe Fassett

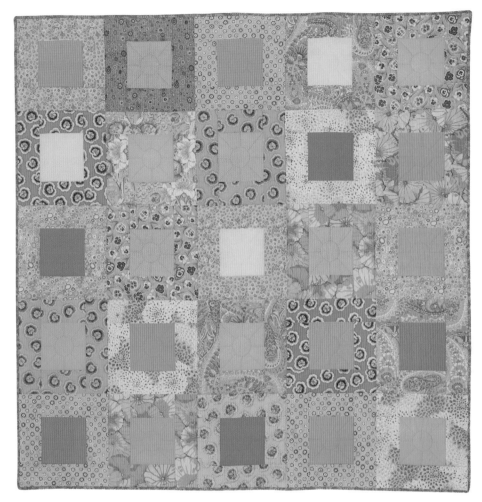

The sunny prints surrounding bright shot cottons give this simple-to-make quilt a brilliant aspect that should light up any room.

SIZE OF QUILT
The finished quilt will measure approx. 75in × 75in (190.5cm × 190.5cm).

MATERIALS
Patchwork Fabrics:
ROMAN GLASS
Gold	GP01GD: ⅜yd (35cm)	

PAPERWEIGHT
Lime	GP20LM: ½yd (45cm)

LOTUS LEAF
Jade	GP29JA: ⅜yd (35cm)
Yellow	GP29YE: ½yd (45cm)

LILIES
Lime	GP45LM: ⅜yd (35cm)

AURICULA
Gold	GP52GD: ⅝yd (60cm)

ORGANIC DOTS
Spring	GP53SP: ½yd (45cm)

DAHLIA BLOOMS
Spring	GP54SP: ⅝yd (60cm)

PAISLEY JUNGLE
Lime	GP60LM: ⅝yd (60cm)

PANSY
Sunny	PJ01SY: ½yd (45cm)

GERANIUM LEAF
Lilac	PJ05LI: ½yd (45cm)
Mint	PJ05MT: ⅜yd (35cm)
Yellow	PJ05YE: ½yd (45cm)

SHOT COTTON
Tangerine	SC11: ¼yd (25cm)
Rosy	SC32: ¼yd (25cm)
Watermelon	SC33: ¼yd (25cm)
Lemon	SC34: ¼yd (25cm)
Sunshine	SC35: ¼yd (25cm)
Apple	SC39: ¼yd (25cm)
Butter	SC64: ¼yd (25cm)

Backing Fabric: 4¾yds (4.35m)
We suggest the following fabrics for backing:
PAISLEY JUNGLE Tangerine, GP60TN
LOTUS LEAF Jade, GP29JA

Binding:
CORAL LEAF
Green	PJ12GN: ⅝yd (60cm)

Batting:
83in × 83in (211cm × 211cm).

Quilting thread:
Pale yellow machine quilting thread
Perlé embroidery threads to match the Shot Cotton block centres.

PATCH SHAPES
See Earthy Frames Quilt.

CUTTING OUT

Cut the fabric in the order stated.

Squares: Cut 8in (20.25cm) squares. Cut 5 in SC35, SC64, 4 in SC39, 3 in SC32, SC33, SC34 and 2 in SC11.

Long Rectangles: Cut 4¼in (10.75cm) strips across the width of the fabric. Cut 4¼in × 15½in (10.75cm × 39.5cm) rectangles. Cut 6 in GP52GD, GP54SP, GP60LM, 4 in GP20LM, GP29YE, GP53SP, PJ01SY, PJ05LI, PJ05YE, 2 in GP01GD, GP29JA, GP45LM and PJ05MT. Reserve the left over strips for the Short Rectangles.

Short Rectangles: Cut 4¼in (10.75cm) strips across the width of the fabric. Cut 4¼in × 8in (10.75cm × 20.25cm) rectangles. Also use the leftovers from the Long Rectangles. Cut 6 in GP52GD, GP54SP, GP60LM, 4 in GP20LM, GP29YE, GP53SP, PJ01SY, PJ05LI, PJ05YE, 2 in GP01GD, GP29JA, GP45LM and PJ05MT.

Binding: Cut 8 strips 2½in (6.5cm) wide × width of fabric in PJ12GN.

Backing: Cut 2 pieces 44in × 83in (112cm × 211cm) in backing fabric.

MAKING THE BLOCKS

Use a ¼in (6mm) seam allowance throughout. Referring to the quilt assembly diagram for fabric placement, piece 25 blocks as shown in the block assembly diagram for Earthy Frames Quilt on page 62. Note that the position of the long and short rectangles alternates across the whole quilt.

MAKING THE QUILT

See Earthy Frames Quilt instructions.

FINISHING THE QUILT

Press the quilt top. Seam the backing pieces using a ¼in (6mm) seam allowance to form a piece approx. 83in × 83in (211cm × 211cm). Layer the quilt top, batting and backing and baste together (see page 139). Using perlé cotton to match the centre squares of each block hand quilt a sunburst design on each square as shown in the quilting diagram. Then, using pale yellow machine quilting thread, machine quilt the design shown in the quilting diagram and also in the ditch as shown. Trim the quilt edges and attach the binding (see page 140).

Quilting Diagram

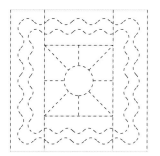

Quilt Assembly Diagram

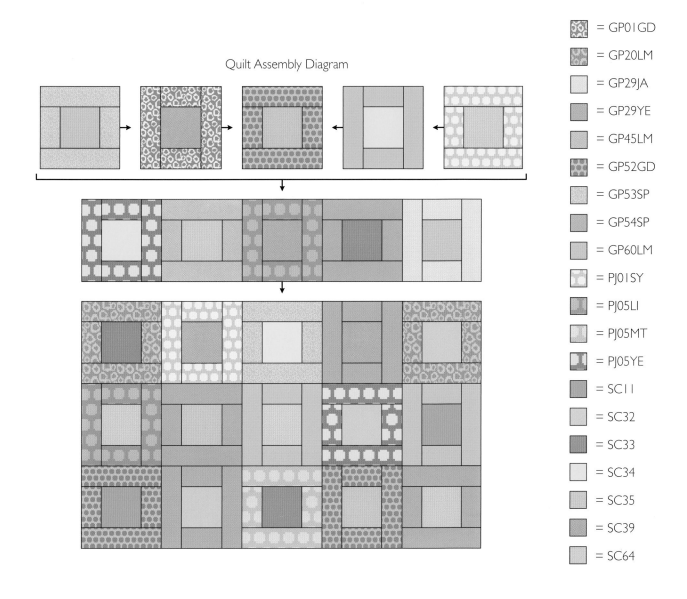

= GP01GD

= GP20LM

= GP29JA

= GP29YE

= GP45LM

= GP52GD

= GP53SP

= GP54SP

= GP60LM

= PJ01SY

= PJ05LI

= PJ05MT

= PJ05YE

= SC11

= SC32

= SC33

= SC34

= SC35

= SC39

= SC64

Goes Around Comes Around Quilt ★★

MARY MASHUTA

Mary revives a quilt block she discovered in the mid 1980's. She also returns to two of her favourite print types, stripes and paisleys. And she says 'yes' to her favourite pieced stripe border, which is much easier than it looks. You can truly say 'what goes around comes around'.

SIZE OF QUILT
The finished quilt will measure approx. 72½in x 72½in (184.25cm x 184.25cm).

MATERIALS
Patchwork and Border Fabrics:
PAISLEY JUNGLE
Green   GP60GN: ½yd (45cm)

Rust   GP60RU: 1¾yds (1.6m)
Tangerine   GP60TN: 1½yds (1.4m)
WOVEN HAZE STRIPE
Persimmon   HZS01: ¾ yd (70cm)
Sunshine   HZS06: ⅜yd (35cm)
SHOT COTTON
Tangerine   SC11: ¼yd (25cm)

Grass   SC27: ¼yd (25cm)
Sunshine   SC35: ¼yd (25cm)
Apple   SC39: ¼yd (25cm)
SINGLE IKAT FEATHERS
Earth   SIF02: 1¼yds (1.15m)

Backing Fabric: 4½ yds (4.1m)
We suggest these fabrics for backing:

PAISLEY JUNGLE Tangerine, GP60TN
WOVEN HAZE STRIPE Sunshine, HZS06

Binding:
WOVEN HAZE STRIPE
Terracotta   HZS10: ⅝yd (60cm)

Batting:
80in × 80in (203cm × 203cm).

Quilting thread:
Machine quilting thread in dark green, gold and a toning shade.

Templates:

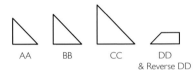

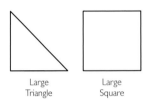

PATCH SHAPES
The main blocks are made using 1 triangle patch shape (Template AA) and 1 lozenge patch shape (Template DD & Reverse DD). The blocks are set 'on point' alternated with 1 Large Square patch shape, cut to size. The edges of the quilt centre are completed using 1 Large Triangle patch shape cut to size, and the corners are filled with 1 triangle patch shape (Template CC). The quilt centre is surrounded by a pieced border, made using 2 triangle patch shapes (Template BB and CC) which are pieced into blocks. Finally the quilt is finished with an outer border, with corner posts. Note: Templates BB and CC do not have grain lines as the grain is different depending on the fabric, i.e. print or stripe.

CUTTING OUT
Important Information:
Please read carefully before cutting the stripe fabrics.
1. Stripe pattern placement is very important graphically. (Don't worry about the grainline.) Consult the quilt assembly diagram and remember for striped fabrics you can always turn your patch over as they are reversible.
2. Open out the stripe fabric and cut one layer at a time.
3. Use a gridded ruler to get the first accurate cut across the fabric by lining up the stripe lines with ruler lines.
4. Keep checking that your cutting line is still perpendicular to the ruler edge as you cut. Take time to correct, if necessary. This extra effort is worth it, and a little extra fabric has been allowed for you to 'true up' your stripes.
5. If the stripe lines need to run down the long side of the triangle you will be cutting strips down the length of the fabric, then placing the long side of the triangle against the cut edge of the fabric.

Cut the fabric in the order stated.
Large Triangle: Cut 3 × 12½in (31.75cm) squares then cut each square twice diagonally to make 4 triangles. This will ensure the long side of the triangles will not have a bias edge. Total 12 Large Triangles in GP60TN.
Large Square: Cut 8½in (21.5cm) wide strips across the width of the fabric. Each strip will give you 4 patches per 45in (114cm) wide

Cutting Diagram

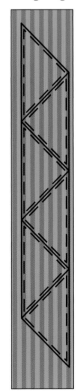

Main Block Assembly Diagrams

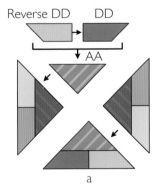

a

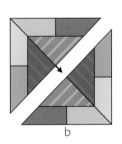

b

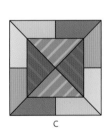

c

Border Block Assembly Diagrams

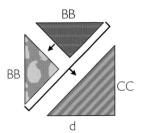

d

e

fabric. Cut 13 in GP60TN (includes 4 for outer border). Reserve the remaining fabric for template CC.

Template BB: For fabric GP60GN. Cut 4⅞in (12.5cm) wide strips across the width of the fabric. Each strip will give you 16 patches per 45in (114cm) wide fabric. Cut 4⅞in (12.5cm) squares, cut each square diagonally to form 2 triangles using the template as a guide. Cut a total of 32 triangles.
For fabric HZS01, see note 5 above: Cut 3½in (9cm) strips down the length of the fabric lining up the ruler along the stripes. Don't worry whether the stripes are light or dark in this case. Place the template with the long side against the cut edge of the strip turning it 180 degrees for each cut. Cut a total of 32 triangles.

Template AA: Cut 4⅜in (11.25cm) wide strips across the width of the fabric. Each strip will give you 18 patches per 45in (114cm) wide fabric. Cut 4⅜in (11.25cm) squares, cut each square diagonally to form 2 triangles using the template as a guide. Important: Refer to the quilt assembly diagram for stripe direction before you cut the squares diagonally. Cut 32 in HZS01 and HZS06.

Template CC: For fabric GP60TN. Use the left over fabric from cutting Large Squares. Cut 2 × 6½in (16.5cm) squares, cut each square diagonally to form 2 triangles using the template as a guide, total 4 triangles.
For fabric GP60GN. Cut 2 × 6½in (16.5cm) squares, cut each square diagonally to form 2 triangles using the template as a guide, total 4 triangles.
For fabric SIF02. Beginning at the selvedge edge cut 6 strips parallel to the edge approximately 6in (15.25cm) wide, making sure that each strip has 6 whole dark stripes across the width of the strip. Place the template with the long side against a dark stripe, as shown in the cutting diagram, turning it 180 degrees for each cut. Cut a total of 36 triangles.

Template DD & Reverse DD: Cut 2in (5cm) wide strips across the width of the fabric. Each strip will give you 10 patches per 45in (114cm) wide fabric. Cut 32 in SC27 and SC39. reverse the template and cut 32 in SC11 and SC35.

Outer Border: Cut from the length of the fabric 4 strips 58in × 8½in (147.5cm × 21.5cm) in GP60RU. These are slightly long, trim as necessary.

Binding: Cut 8⅜yds (7.7m) of 2½in (6.5cm) wide bias binding in HZS10.

Backing: Cut 2 pieces 40½in × 90in (103cm × 229cm) in backing fabric.

Important Information:
Please read carefully before sewing.
There are many bias edges in this quilt, Mary considered this and deliberately cut adjoining pieces on grain where possible. When stitching segments place the bias edge next to the feed dogs. Sometimes you must join bias edges, just be gentle and try not to stretch the edges as you feed them through the machine. Using the point of a seam ripper will help you guide the pieces.

MAKING THE QUILT CENTRE
Use a ¼in (6mm) seam allowance throughout. Referring to the quilt assembly diagram for fabric placement piece 16 identical blocks following main block assembly diagrams a and b, the finished block can be seen in diagram c. Lay out the blocks alternating with the large squares and filling in the sides with the large triangles. The corners are completed with the template CC triangles.

MAKING THE PIECED BORDERS
Referring to the quilt assembly diagram for fabric placement piece 32 identical blocks

following border block assembly diagram d, the finished block can be seen in diagram e. Piece into 4 rows of 8 blocks. Join a row to each side of the quilt centre. Take 8 template CC triangles and make 4 pieced corner posts. Join a corner post to each end of the top and bottom borders and then join to the quilt centre.

ADDING THE OUTER BORDER
Measure the quilt and trim the out borders to fit. Join the side outer borders to the quilt centre. Join a corner post (Large Square) to each end of the top and bottom borders and then join to the quilt centre as shown in the quilt assembly diagram.

FINISHING THE QUILT
Press the quilt top. Seam the backing pieces using a ¼in (6mm) seam allowance to form a piece approx 80in × 80in (203cm × 203cm). Layer the quilt top, batting and backing and baste together (see page 139). Using a walking foot, machine quilt all the main vertical, horizontal and diagonal seams with toning thread. Refer to the quilting diagram for additional quilting which can be done in cotton or rayon thread. Use dark green for the quilt centre and outer border corner posts and gold for the outer borders. Trim the quilt edges and attach the binding (see page 140).

Quilting Diagram

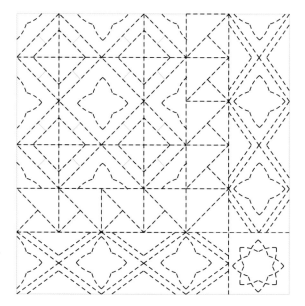

Quilt Assembly Diagram

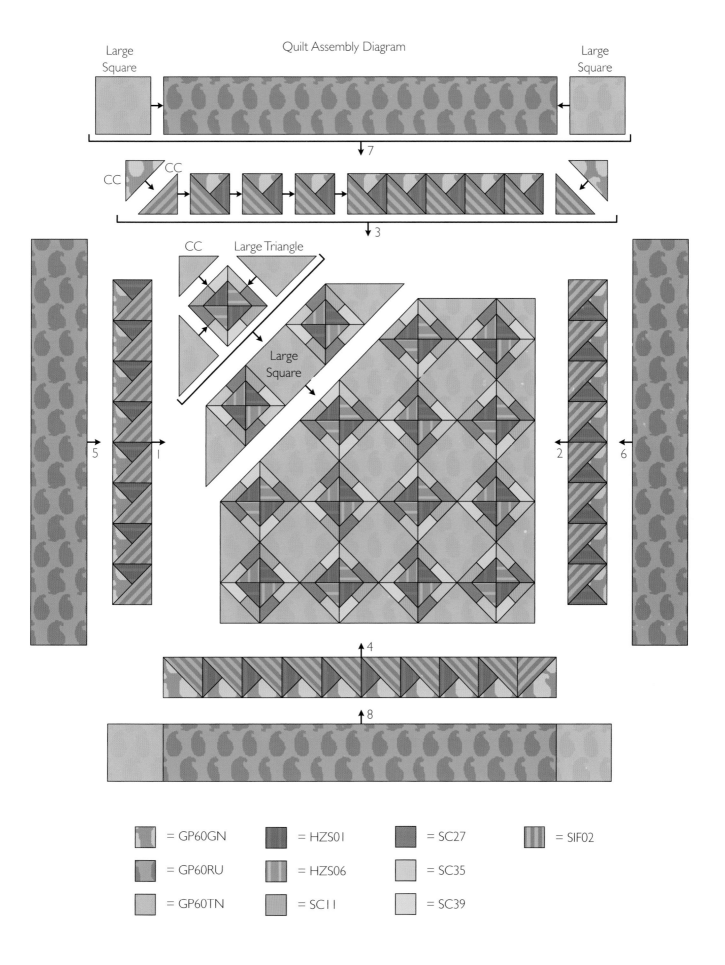

Large Square

Large Square

CC CC

CC Large Triangle

Large Square

= GP60GN
= GP60RU
= GP60TN

= HZS01
= HZS06
= SC11

= SC27
= SC35
= SC39

= SIF02

Chelsea Quilt ★★

PAULINE SMITH

Chelsea is fun to make, simple stylized flowers are appliquéd liberally across the pieced quilt centre.

SIZE OF QUILT
The finished quilt will measure approx. 45¾in x 51¾in (116.25cm x 131.5cm).

MATERIALS
Patchwork and Border Fabrics:
LOTUS LEAF
Umber   GP29UM: ¾yd (70cm)
PAPER FANS
Ochre   GP57OC: ¼yd (25cm)
GUINEA FLOWER

Brown   GP59BR: ⅜yd (35cm)
WOVEN HAZE STRIPE
Mustard   HZS02: ⅜yd (35cm)
PANSIES
Oxblood   PJ01OX: ¼yd (25cm)
SHOT COTTON
Brick   SC58: ¼yd (25cm)
SINGLE IKAT FEATHERS
Earth   SIF02: ¼yd (25cm)
SINGLE IKAT WASH
Banana   SIW03: ⅞yd (80cm)

Appliqué Fabrics:
Note: For some fabrics only a tiny amount is needed, so you could use scraps from other Rowan projects.
CHICKEN SCRATCH
Fuchsia   CM05FU: ⅛yd (15cm)
SHIRT STRIPES
Soft   GP51SF: ⅜yd (35cm)
GUINEA FLOWER
Yellow   GP59YE: ⅛yd (15cm)
WOVEN HAZE STRIPE

| Pine | HZS19: ⅛yd (15cm) |
| Grape | HZS22: ¼yd (25cm) |

SHOT COTTON

Thunder	SC06: ⅛yd (15cm)
Persimmon	SC07: ⅛yd (15cm)
Pomegranate	SC09: ⅛yd (15cm)
Lilac	SC14: ⅛yd (15cm)
Brick	SC58: Use leftover from patchwork fabric.

SINGLE IKAT FEATHERS

| Earth | SIF02: Use leftover from patchwork fabric. |

Backing Fabric: 3⅛yds (2.9m)
We suggest these fabrics for backing:
PANSIES Oxblood, PJ01OX
LOTUS LEAF Umber, GP29UM
WOVEN HAZE STRIPE Mustard, HZS02

Binding:
PANSIES
Oxblood PJ01OX: ½yd (45cm) or use leftover from backing.

Batting:
54in x 60in (137cm x 152.5cm).

Quilting thread:
Ochre machine quilting thread.
Dark red and mauve embroidery threads.

PATCH SHAPES
The background of this pretty quilt is pieced from a selection of rectangles, cut to size. These are pieced into 3 columns, then joined to form the quilt centre. Simple hand appliqué is then added to the background. Templates are provided for flowers, leaf and small vase shape. The larger vase is a simple rectangle, cut to size. The flower stems are also cut to size. The quilt is finished with a border with corner posts cut to size.

CUTTING OUT
Rectangle 1: Cut 7¾in x 20¾in (19.75cm x 52.75cm) in SIW03.
Rectangle 2: Cut 7¾in x 6in (19.75cm x 15.25cm) in HZS02.
Rectangle 3: Cut 7¾in x 7½in (19.75cm x 19cm) in GP57OC.
Rectangle 4: Cut 7¾in x 8½in (19.75cm x 21.5cm) in SC58.
Rectangle 5: Cut 12in x 8¾in (30.5cm x 22.25cm) in HZS02.
Rectangle 6: Cut 12in x 8¼in (30.5cm x 21cm) in GP57OC.
Rectangle 7: Cut 12in x 8¼in (30.5cm x 21cm) in PJ01OX.
Rectangle 8: Cut 12in x 11in (30.5cm x 28cm) in GP59BR.

Rectangle 9: Cut 12in x 7in (30.5cm x 17.75cm) in SIF02.
Rectangle 10: Cut 16½in x 10¼in (42cm x 26cm) in GP59BR.
Rectangle 11: Cut 16½in x 5in (42cm x 12.75cm) in SIF02.
Rectangle 12: Cut 12½in x 27in (31.75cm x 68.5cm) in SIW03.
Rectangle 13: Cut 4½in x 27in (11.5cm x 68.5cm) in SC58.

Border: Cut 2 strips 41¼in x 6in (104.75cm x 15.25cm) for the quilt sides and 2 strips 35¼in x 6in (89.5cm x 15.25cm) for the quilt top and bottom in GP29UM. Also cut 4 x 6in (15.25cm) squares for the corner posts in GP59BR.

Appliqué Shapes:
Large Circle: Cut 2 in SC14.
Medium Circle: Cut 3 in SC07, SC06, 2 in CM05FU, 1 in SC58 and SC09.
Small Circle: Cut 4 in SC06, 1 in SC07 and SC09.
Flower Centres: Cut 5 in HZS19, 4 in SC09, 3 in SC07 and 1 in CM05FU using the flower centre template. Also fussy cut 5 pansies from GP59YE.
Leaf: Cut 6 in SC06, 3 in GP51SF and 2 in HZS19.
Vases: Using the vase template cut 2 in HZS22, note the stripe direction is horizontal. Also cut a rectangle 7½in x 5¾in (19cm x 14.75cm) in SIF02, note the stripe direction is vertical.
Flower Stems: Using the design elements of the fabric as a guide cut varying lengths and widths of the fabric ranging from 4in to 12½in (10cm to 31.75cm) in length and ⅞in to 1¼ in (2.25cm to 3.25cm) in width. Also refer to the photograph.

Binding: Cut 5 strips 2½in (6.5cm) wide x width of fabric in PJ01OX.

Backing: Cut 2 pieces 30½in x 54in (77.5cm x 137cm) in backing fabric.

MAKING THE QUILT CENTRE
Use a ¼in (6mm) seam allowance throughout. Referring to the quilt centre assembly diagram for fabric placement, piece 3 columns as shown in the quilt centre assembly diagram. Join the columns to form the quilt centre.

APPLIQUÉ AND BORDER
Refer to the Patchwork Know How Hand Appliqué section on page 138 for appliqué techniques and to the quilt assembly diagram and photographs for appliqué positioning and fabrics. Press a ¼in (6mm) seam allowance rounds each vase shape. Apply the vases to the quilt centre, leaving the top unstitched for now. Again using a ¼in (6mm) seam allowance, apply the flower stems, tucking the bottoms into the vases as appropriate. Finish

Quilt Centre Assembly Diagram

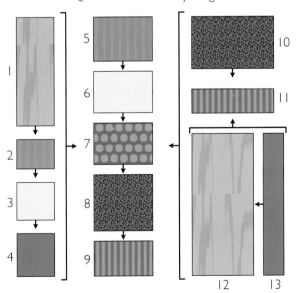

the bottoms of all other stems neatly (the tops will be covered by flowers). Stitch down the top edges of the vases. Make the flowers using the card template method. Apply the centres to the flowers before adding to the quilt centre. Arrange the flowers and stitch into place. Finally add the leaves using the finger pressing method. Add the border as shown in the quilt assembly diagram.

FINISHING THE QUILT

Press the quilt top. Seam the backing pieces using a ¼in (6mm) seam allowance to form a piece approx. 54in x 60in (137cm x 152.5cm). Layer the quilt top, batting and backing and baste together (see page 139). Using Ochre machine quilting thread quilt in the ditch around the rectangle background shapes, quilt the striped background rectangles following the fabric stripes about 1½in (3.75cm) apart. Hand quilt around the flowers using dark red and mauve embroidery threads. Also Pauline embellished the flowers, background fabrics and borders with embroidered French knots and the fussy cut pansy flower centres with blanket stitch. Trim the quilt edges and attach the binding (see page 140).

Quilt Assembly Diagram

	= CM05PK
	= GP29UM
	= GP51SF
	= GP57OC
	= GP59BR
	= GP59YE
	= HZS02
	= HZS19
	= HZS22
	= PJ01OX
	= SC06
	= SC07
	= SC09
	= SC14
	= SC58
	= SIF02
	= SIW03

Gilded Snowballs Quilt ★★★

KAFFE FASSETT

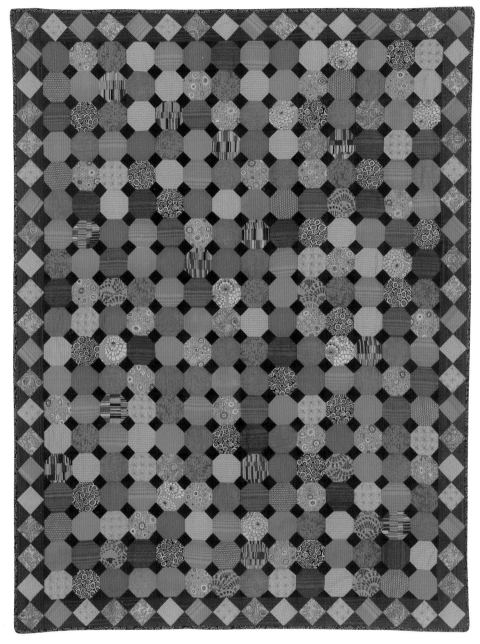

Snowballs is one of my favourite quilt layouts; in this version I've added a pieced border which, finishes off the quilt a treat.

SIZE OF QUILT
The finished quilt will measure approx. 56in × 73½in (142.25cm × 186.75cm).

MATERIALS
Patchwork and Border Fabrics:
LAYERED TWIRLS
Burnt Orange   CM06BO: ⅜yd (35cm)

ROOTLETS
Burnt Orange   CM07BO: ¼yd (25cm)
Mauve   CM07MV: ⅛yd (15cm)
STARSHINE
Mauve   CM08MV: ⅜yd (35cm)
SWIRL MINI
Mauve   CM10MV: ½yd (45cm)
Sea Green   CM10SG: ¼yd (25cm)

ROMAN GLASS
Gold   GP01GD: ⅜yd (35cm)
SHIRT STRIPES
Autumn   GP51AT: ¼yd (25cm)
ORGANIC DOTS
Gold   GP53GD: ¼yd (25cm)
FLOATING FLOWERS
Yellow   GP56YE: ⅛yd (15cm)
PAPER FANS
Ochre   GP57OC: ⅛yd (15cm)
WOVEN HAZE STRIPE
Persimmon   HZS01: ¼yd (25cm)
Pewter   HZS05: ¼yd (25cm)
Sunshine   HZS06: ½yd (45cm)
Ginger   HZS21: ⅞yd (80cm)
SHOT COTTON
Cassis   SC02: ⅝yd (60cm)
Prune/Thunder   SC03/SC06: 1⅛yds (1m)
    (use either)
Tangerine   SC11: ¼yd (25cm)
Sage   SC17: ¼yd (25cm)
Tobacco   SC18: ¼yd (25cm)
Charcoal   SC25: ¼yd (25cm)
Brick   SC58: ¼yd (25cm)
SINGLE IKAT WASH
Red   SIW06: ¼yd (25cm)

Backing Fabric: 3⅝yds (3.3m)
We suggest these fabrics for backing:
FLOATING FLOWERS Brown, GP56BR
ROMAN GLASS Gold, GP01GD
ROOTLETS Mauve, CM07MV

Binding:
ORGANIC DOTS
Brown   GP53BR: ⅝yd (60cm)

Batting:
64in × 82in (162.5cm × 208cm).

Quilting thread:
Toning machine quilting thread.

Templates:

PATCH SHAPES
The centre of this quilt is pieced from a traditional Snowball block, made from an octagon and four triangles, in this case it is made 'the easy way' by using a large square

(Template LL) and 4 small squares (Template MM) for each block. The small squares are placed over the corners of the large squares and stitched diagonally. They are then trimmed and flipped back to replace the corners of the large square. The centre is then surrounded with a pieced border, using a medium square (Template EE) and 2 triangles (Templates NN and OO).

CUTTING OUT
Template LL: Cut 4in (10.25cm) wide strips across the width of the fabric. Each strip will give you 10 patches per 45in (114cm) wide fabric. Cut 28 in GP01GD, 23 in CM10MV, 20 in HZS06, 19 in GP53GD, SC18, 18 in CM07BO, SC58, 15 in HZS01, HZS05, 13 in CM08MV, GP51AT, SIW06, 12 in SC11, 10 in SC17, 9 in CM10SG, GP56YE, 8 in GP57OC and 4 in CM06BO.
Template EE: Cut 3in (7.75cm) wide strips across the width of the fabric. Each strip will give you 14 patches per 45in (114cm) wide fabric. Cut 17 in HZS06, 15 in CM06BO, 13 in CM07MV, CM08MV and 12 in CM10MV.
Template MM: Cut 1½in (3.8cm) wide strips across the width of the fabric. Each strip will give you 28 patches per 45in (114cm) wide fabric. Cut 621 in SC03/SC06, 345 in SC02 and 98 in SC25.
Template OO: Cut a 2⅝in (6.75cm) strip

across the width of the fabric. Cut 8 x 2⅝in (6.75cm) squares, cut each square diagonally to form 2 triangles using the template as a guide, total 16 triangles in HZS21.
Template NN: Cut 2⅜in (6cm) strips down the length of the fabric lining up the ruler along the stripes. Place the template with the long side against the cut edge of the strip turning it 180 degrees for each cut. Cut a total of 132 triangles in HZS21.

Binding: Cut 7 strips 2½in (6.5cm) wide × width of fabric in GP53BR.

Backing: Cut 2 pieces 42in × 64in (106.5cm × 162.5cm) in backing fabric.

MAKING THE BLOCKS
To make the Snowball blocks take one large square (template LL) and four small squares (template MM), using the quilt assembly diagram as a guide to fabric combinations. Place one small square, right sides together onto each corner of the large square, matching the edges carefully as shown in block assembly diagram a. Stitch diagonally across the small squares as shown in diagram b. Trim the corners to a ¼in (6mm) seam allowance and press the corners out (diagram c). Make 266 blocks. When the blocks are joined, the corners should come

together to form 'squares' in the same fabrics.

MAKING THE QUILT CENTRE
Use a ¼in (6mm) seam allowance throughout. Piece the blocks into 19 rows of 14 blocks. Join the rows to form the quilt centre.

MAKING THE PIECED BORDERS
Refer to the quilt assembly diagram for fabric placement and the border assembly diagram for construction details. Piece 2 borders each with 14 medium squares (template EE), 26 template NN triangles and 4 template OO triangles to complete the ends for the quilt top and bottom and 2 borders each with 19 medium squares (template EE) 40 template NN triangles and 4 template OO triangles to complete the ends for the quilt sides. Join to the quilt centre in the order shown in the quilt assembly diagram.

FINISHING THE QUILT
Press the quilt top. Seam the backing pieces using a ¼in (6mm) seam allowance to form a piece approx 64in x 82in (162.5cm × 208cm). Layer the quilt top, batting and backing and baste together (see page 139). Using toning machine quilting thread quilt in the ditch in all seams. Trim the quilt edges and attach the binding (see page 140).

Block Assembly Diagrams

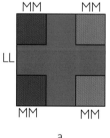 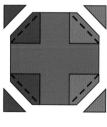 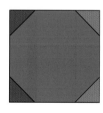

a   b   c

Border Assembly Diagram

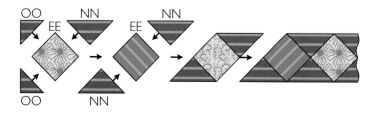

Quilt Assembly Diagram

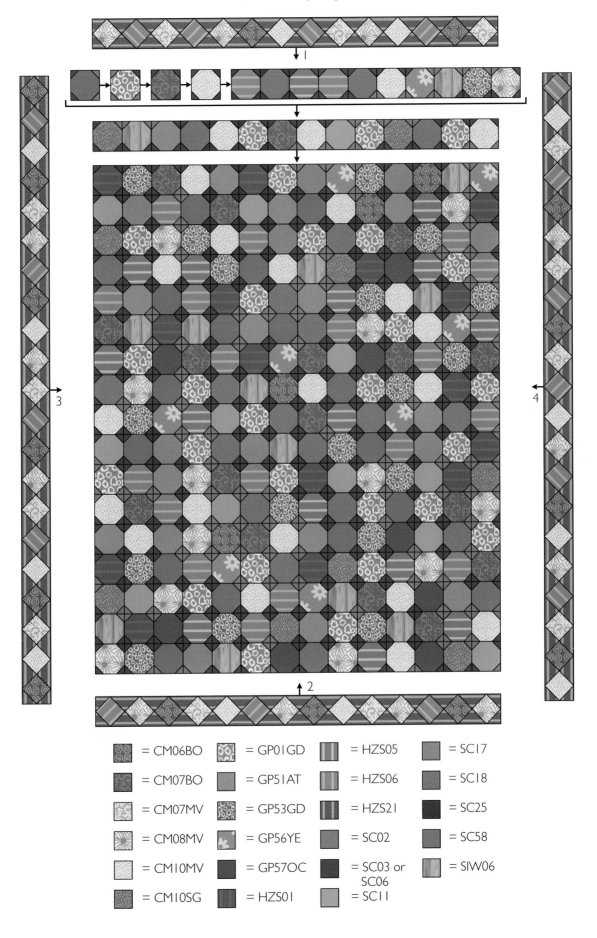

= CM06BO	= GP01GD	= HZS05	= SC17
= CM07BO	= GP51AT	= HZS06	= SC18
= CM07MV	= GP53GD	= HZS21	= SC25
= CM08MV	= GP56YE	= SC02	= SC58
= CM10MV	= GP57OC	= SC03 or SC06	= SIW06
= CM10SG	= HZS01	= SC11	

Brick Bracket Medallion Quilt ★

ROBERTA HORTON

Have your daydreams of making a medallion quilt been stopped by the necessary math calculations? Roberta found the ultimate solution, where wonderful fabrics do all the work of suggesting the complexity of an antique medallion quilt!

SIZE OF QUILT
The finished quilt will measure approx. 57in × 57in (145cm × 145cm).

MATERIALS
Patchwork Fabrics:
OXFORD STRIPES
Blue   AB05BL: ¼yd (25cm)
Okra   AB05OK: ¼yd (25cm)
Olive   AB05OV: ¼yd (25cm)
ROYAL GARDEN

Clay   AB06CY: 1yd (90cm)
this quantity is very generous to allow for fussy cutting.
GOTHIC ROSE
Blue   AB09BL: ⅞yd (80cm)
LOTUS LEAF
Green   GP29GN: ⅛yd (15cm)
Umber   GP29UM: ⅛yd (15cm)
Yellow   GP29YE: ⅛yd (15cm)
FLOATING FLOWERS
Blue   GP56BL: ⅛yd (15cm)

Green   GP56GN: ⅛yd (15cm)
Mauve   GP56MV: ⅛yd (15cm)
Yellow   GP56YE: ⅛yd (15cm)
PAPER FANS
Brown   GP57BR: ⅛yd (15cm)
Ochre   GP57OC: ⅛yd (15cm)
Teal   GP57TE: ⅛yd (15cm)
SAMARKAND
Green   GP58GN: ⅛yd (15cm)
Ochre   GP58OC: ⅛yd (15cm)
Stone   GP58ST: ⅛yd (15cm)

GUINEA FLOWER

Brown   GP59BR: ⅜yd (35cm)
Green   GP59GN: ⅛yd (15cm)
Yellow   GP59YE: ⅛yd (15cm)

Backing Fabric: 3¾yds (3.4m)
We suggest these fabrics for backing:
HENNA PAISLEY Okra, AB04OK
LOTUS LEAF Green, GP29GN

Binding:
PAPER FANS
Green   GP57GN: ⅝yd (60cm)

Batting:
65in x 65in (165cm x 165cm).

Quilting thread:
Machine quilting threads in rust, green, yellow and invisible.

PATCH SHAPES

Based around a square centre panel this quilt has a succession of plain and pieced borders. The pieced borders are formed from a simple 'brick' rectangle patch shape. The corners of the pieced borders are completed using 1 square patch shape (borders 2 and 6) and 2 additional rectangle patch shapes (border 4), these form visual 'brackets' at the corners. All are cut to size and no templates are provided for these very simple shapes. See the quilt assembly diagram for details.

CUTTING OUT

Centre Panel: Cut 1 square 21½in x 21½in (54.5cm x 54.5cm) in AB06CY. Refer to the quilt photographs for guidance with design position. A generous amount of fabric has been allowed so you can centre the fabric design to best effect.
Pieced Borders (2, 4 and 6): Cut 3½in (9cm) strips across the width of the fabric. From these cut 3½in x 6½in (9cm x 16.5cm) rectangles. Cut 4 in GP29GN, GP29UM, GP29YE, GP56BL, GP56GN, GP56MV, GP56YE, GP57BR, GP57OC, GP57TE, GP58GN, GP58OC, GP58ST, GP59BR, GP59GN and GP59YE.
Corner Bracket Rectangles and Squares: All from fabric GP59BR, cut 3½in (9cm) strips across the width of the fabric. From these cut 4 rectangles 3½in x 5in (9cm x 12.75cm) and 4 rectangles 3½in x 2in (9cm x 5cm) for border 4. Cut 8 squares 3½in x 3½in (9cm x 9cm) for borders 2 and 6.
Border 1: Cut 2in (5cm) strips across the width of the fabric. From these cut 2 strips 2in x 21½in (5cm x 54.5cm) for the quilt top

and bottom and 2 strips 2in x 24½in (5cm x 62.25cm) for the quilt sides in AB05OK.
Border 3: Cut 2in (5cm) strips across the width of the fabric. From these cut 2 strips 2in x 30½in (5cm x 77.5cm) for the quilt top and bottom and 2 strips 2in x 33½in (5cm x 85cm) for the quilt sides in AB05BL.
Border 5: Cut 2in (5cm) strips across the width of the fabric. From these cut 2 strips 2in x 39½in (5cm x 100.5cm) for the quilt top and bottom and 2 strips 2in x 42½in (5cm x 108cm) for the quilt sides in AB05OV.
Border 7: Cut 6 strips 5in (12.75cm) x width of the fabric. Join as necessary and cut 2 strips 5in x 48½in (12.75cm x 123.25cm) for the quilt top and bottom, and 2 strips 5in x 57½in (12.75cm x 146cm) for the quilt sides in AB09BL.

Binding: Cut 7 strips 2½in (6.5cm) wide x width of fabric in GP57GN.

Backing: Cut 1 piece 42in x 65in (107cm x 165cm) and 1 piece 24in x 65in (61cm x 165cm) in backing fabric.

MAKING THE QUILT

Use a ¼in (6mm) seam allowance throughout. Referring to the quilt assembly diagram for fabric placement piece borders 2, 4 and 6, adding the corner bracket shapes as shown in the quilt assembly diagram. Then starting with Border 1 join the strips, first to the top and bottom of the quilt, then to the quilt sides, as indicated in the quilt assembly diagram. Continue in the same way until all 7 borders have been joined.

FINISHING THE QUILT

Press the quilt top. Seam the backing pieces using a ¼in (6mm) seam allowance to form a piece approx. 65in x 65in (165cm x 165cm). Layer the quilt top, batting and backing and baste together (see page 139). Machine quilt as shown in the quilting diagram. Use invisible quilting thread for the seams that separate the borders. Use rust thread in the centre medallion area. Use yellow thread for border 2, green for borders 4 and 7, and rust for border 6. Trim the quilt edges and attach the binding (see page 140).

Quilting Diagram

Quilt Assembly Diagram

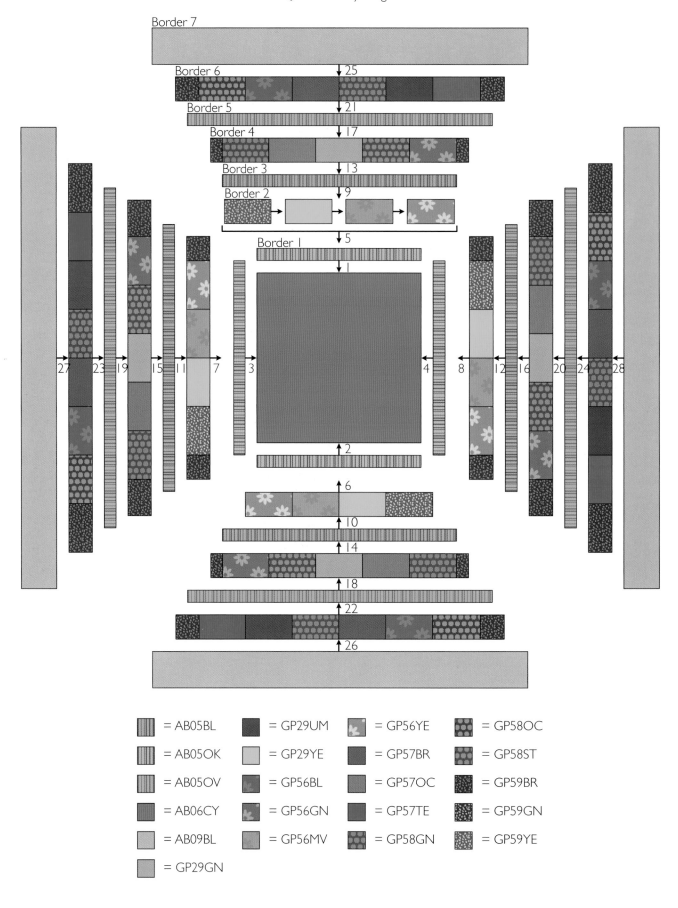

▦ = AB05BL	■ = GP29UM	▦ = GP56YE	▦ = GP58OC
▦ = AB05OK	□ = GP29YE	■ = GP57BR	▦ = GP58ST
▦ = AB05OV	▦ = GP56BL	▦ = GP57OC	▦ = GP59BR
▦ = AB06CY	▦ = GP56GN	■ = GP57TE	▦ = GP59GN
▦ = AB09BL	▦ = GP56MV	▦ = GP58GN	▦ = GP59YE
▦ = GP29GN			

Big Star Quilt ★★★

BRANDON MABLY

I was inspired by a bold up scale Star quilt from the 1850's in Amish colourings. I took six fabrics and slightly heightened the colourings by adding the sharp 'Auricula' indigo and Kaffe's big 'Paisley Jungle' against the bold tumbling blocks that radiate around the smouldering red of the centre star.

SIZE OF QUILT
The finished quilt will measure approx.
66½in x 63in (169cm x 160cm).

MATERIALS
Patchwork Fabrics:
CHICKEN SCRATCH
Black   CM05BK: 1¾yds (1.6m)
Red   CM05RD: ⅜yd (35cm)
AURICULA

Indigo   GP52IN: ¾ yd (70cm)
Red   GP52RD: 1⅛yds (1m)
FLOATING FLOWERS
Brown   GP56BR: ¾ yd (70cm)
PAISLEY JUNGLE
Purple   GP60PU: ¾ yd (70cm)

Backing Fabric: 4yds (3.7m)
We suggest these fabrics for backing:

PAISLEY JUNGLE Rust, GP60RU
AURICULA Red, GP52RD

Binding:
FLOATING FLOWERS
Brown   GP56BR: ⅝yd (60cm)

Batting:
74in x 71in (188cm x 180.5cm).

Quilting thread:
Red and black hand quilting thread.

Templates:

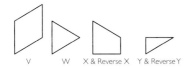

V   W   X & Reverse X   Y & Reverse Y

PATCH SHAPES
A large diamond patch shape (Template V) is used to form 8 large star blocks (Block A) which form the centre of this striking quilt. The quilt edges are completed with 3 further blocks. Block B completes the quilt sides and uses template V, along with an equilateral triangle patch shape (Template W). Block C completes the quilt top and bottom and uses template V and a lozenge patch shape (Template X & Reverse X), this shape is reversed in some positions. Finally, Block D (and reverse D) uses templates V, X & Reverse X and a triangle patch shape (Template Y & Reverse Y), this shape is reversed in some positions.

CUTTING OUT
Template V: Cut 5¾in (14.5cm) strips across the width of the fabric. Each strip will give you 5 patches per 45in (114cm) wide fabric. Cut 42 in CM05BK, 18 in GP51IN, GP56BR, GP60PU, 12 in GP52RD and 6 in CM05RD.
Template W: Cut 6in (15.25cm) strips across the width of the fabric. Cut 4 in CM05BK. Reserve leftover strip and trim for template Y & reverse Y.
Template X & Reverse X: Cut 5¾in (14.5cm) strips across the width of the fabric. Each strip will give you 8 patches per 45in (114cm) wide fabric. Cut 10 in GP52RD, reverse the template and cut a further 10 in GP52RD.
Template Y & Reverse Y: Trim the leftover strip from Template W to 3¾in (9.5cm) and cut 2 in CM05BK, reverse the template and cut a further 2 in CM05BK.

Binding: Cut 7 strips 2½in (6.5cm) wide × width of fabric in GP56BR.

Backing: Cut 1 piece 42in × 71in (106.5cm × 180.5cm) and 1 piece 33in × 71in (84cm × 180.5cm) in backing fabric.

MAKING THE BLOCKS
Use a ¼in (6mm) seam allowance throughout. Referring to the quilt assembly

Block A Assembly Diagrams

Block B Assembly Diagrams

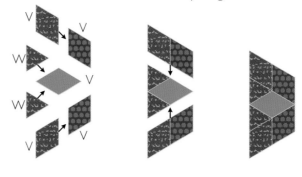

Block C Assembly Diagrams

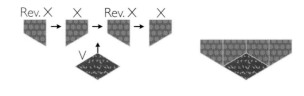

Block D & Reverse D Assembly Diagrams

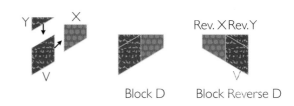

Block D   Block Reverse D

diagram for fabric placement piece 8 × Block A, 2 × Block B, 4 × Block C, 2 × Block D and 2 × Block Reverse D, as shown in block assembly diagrams. Use the inset seam method of piecing as shown in the Patchwork Know How section on page 138.

MAKING THE QUILT
Join the blocks to form the quilt following the numbered stages in the quilt assembly diagram. Again use the inset seam method to join the sections.

FINISHING THE QUILT
Press the quilt top. Seam the backing pieces using a ¼in (6mm) seam allowance to form a piece approx. 74in × 71in (188cm × 180.5cm). Layer the quilt top, batting and backing and baste together (see page 139). Using black hand quilting thread quilt in the ditch around all the CM05BK fabric patches, then echo quilt each patch ¼in (6mm) from the seams. Quilt a line to highlight the black hexagon shapes 2in (5cm) from the seams. Using red hand quilting thread quilt all the other fabric patches in the ditch and ¼in (6mm) from the seams. Along the top and bottom edges quilt zig zag lines 2in (5cm) from the seams. Trim the quilt edges and attach the binding (see page 140).

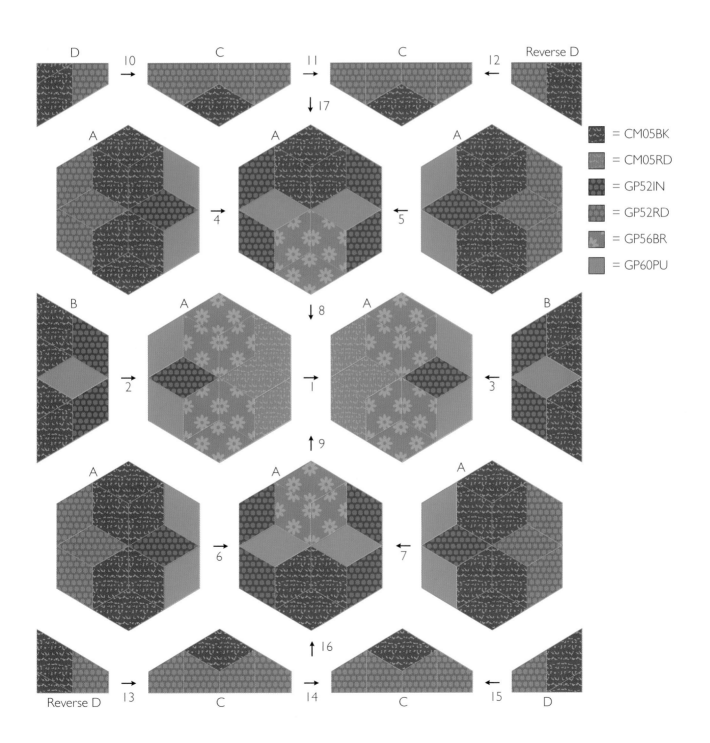

= CM05BK
= CM05RD
= GP52IN
= GP52RD
= GP56BR
= GP60PU

Framed Jar Quilt ★★★

KAFFE FASSETT

When I first designed the blue and white prints in this patchwork, I thought of using them in just this way. The ginger jar is easy to appliqué using the freezer paper method, which gives an accurate shape and makes for easy handling.

SIZE OF QUILT

The finished quilt will measure approx. 80in × 80in (203cm × 203cm).

MATERIALS
Patchwork and Appliqué Fabrics:
HENNA PAISLEY
Okra   AB04OK: ¼yd (25cm)
FULL MOON POLKA DOT
Slate   AB13SE: ½yd (45cm)
TREE PEONY
Sky   AB18SK: ½yd (45cm)
MOSAIC
Teal   CM19TE: ¼yd (25cm)
MUMS
Blue   CM20BL: ¼yd (25cm)
VERBENA
Powder Blue   GP61PB: ¼yd (25cm)
MINTON
Blue   GP63BL: ⅞yd (80cm)
Lavender   GP63LV: 1⅛yds (1m)
Teal   GP63TE: ½yd (45cm)
POTENTILLA
Blue   GP64BL: ⅜yd (35cm)
Pink   GP64PK: ¾yd (70cm)
CORAL LEAF
Blue   PJ12BL: ½yd (45cm)
SHOT COTTON
Ecru   SC24: ¼yd (25cm)
Blush   SC28: 1½yds (1.4m)
Sky   SC62: ¼yd (25cm)
SINGLE IKAT WASH
Lavender   SIW05: ¾yd (70cm)

Backing Fabric: 5yds (4.6m)
We suggest these fabrics for backing:
PAPER FANS Cream, GP57CM
POTENTILLA Pink, GP64PK
TREE PEONY Sky, AB18SK

Binding:
HOLLYHOCKS
Blue   PJ09BL: ⅝yd (60cm)

Batting:
88in × 88in (223.5cm × 223.5cm).

Quilting Thread:
Variegated machine quilting thread in pastel (Coats 883 Sherbet) and blue/green (Coats 851 Sea Mist).

Other Materials:
Freezer Paper.

Templates:

GG   HH   JJ   KK & Reverse KK

PATCH SHAPES

The quilt is formed around a central appliquéd panel surrounded by 6 borders. The central panel is square with a hand appliquéd ginger jar (Framed Jar Quilt Appliqué Jar and Lid templates are printed at 50% of real size, to use scale them up 200% on a photocopier). Borders 1, 3 and 5 are simple borders with corner posts cut to size. Borders 2, 4 and 6 are pieced using 4 triangle templates (Template GG, HH, JJ and KK & reverse KK), these borders also have corner posts, cut to size. You will find half template HH on page 134. Take a large piece of paper, fold, place the edge of template HH on the fold, trace around the shape and cut out. Open out for the complete template.

CUTTING OUT

To reduce waste we suggest drawing round the templates onto the reverse of the fabrics for the best fit before cutting. Note: Cutting strips the full width of the fabric would be very wasteful and we have not allowed enough fabric for this method.

Centre Panel: Cut 1 × 18½in (47cm) square in GP64PK.

Appliqué Shapes: Note: the templates do NOT include a seam allowance.
Cut each template (1 Jar and 1 Lid) in freezer paper, press the shiny side onto the reverse of fabric PJ12BL and cut out ¼in (6mm) OUTSIDE the freezer paper.

Border 1: Cut 4 strips 4in × 18½in (10cm × 47cm) in GP63BL and 4 × 4in (10cm) squares for corner posts in GP64BL.

Border 2: Using Template GG cut 7 in GP63LV, 5 in SC62, 4 in AB04OK, AB13SE, CM19TE, GP63TE, GP64PK, 3 in SC24, SC28 and 2 in AB18SK. Also cut 4 × 5½in (14cm) squares for corner posts in GP63BL.

Border 3: Cut 4 strips 5½in × 35½in (14cm × 90.25cm) in SIW05 and 4 × 5½in (14cm) squares for corner posts in GP64BL.

Border 4: Using Template HH cut 8 in SC28, 6 in GP63TE, GP64PK, 4 in AB13SE, AB18SK, CM20BL, GP61PB, GP63BL, 2 in AB04OK, CM19TE, GP63LV and PJ12BL. Also fussy cut 4 × 8in (20.25cm) squares for corner posts in AB18SK, centring the square on one of the large flower motifs.

Border 5: Cut 6 strips 4½in (11.5cm) wide × width of the fabric in GP63LV. Join strips as necessary and cut 4 strips 4½in × 60½in (11.5cm × 153.75cm). Cut 4 × 4½in (11.5cm) squares for corner posts in GP64BL.

Border 6: Using Template JJ cut 64 in SC28, 10 in GP63BL, 9 in AB18SK, PJ12BL, 8 in GP61PB, 7 in CM20BL, 6 in AB13SE, GP63TE, 5 in CM19TE, GP64BL and 3 in GP64PK.
Using Template KK & Reverse KK cut 4 in SC28, reverse the template and cut 4 more in SC28. Also cut 4 × 6½in (16.5cm) squares for corner posts in GP63BL.

Binding: Cut 8 strips 2½in (6.5cm) wide × width of fabric in PJ09BL.

Backing: Cut 2 pieces 44in × 88in (112cm × 203.5cm) in backing fabric.

MAKING THE CENTRE PANEL

Working first on the jar press the seam allowance to the reverse and baste all around except the top edge as this will be covered by the lid, you can snip the seam allowance at curves and points to allow it to lay flat. Carefully position the jar on the background (leaving room for the lid). Appliqué the jar into place with invisible stitches, see the Patchwork Know How, Freezer paper section on page 139 for additional information. Appliqué the lid in the same way slightly overlapping the jar. Turn the panel to the reverse and cut away the backing behind the appliqué to within ¼in (6mm) of the stitching line. Carefully remove the basting threads and peel off the freezer paper.

Block Assembly Diagram

ADDING BORDERS 1 – 3

Use a ¼in (6mm) seam allowance throughout. Refer to the Border 1 – 3 assembly diagram for fabric placement. Add border 1 as shown in the assembly diagram, sides first, then after adding a corner block to the ends of each, add the top and bottom borders.

For Border 2 piece a total of 20 blocks as shown in the block assembly diagram using template GG triangles. Stitch into 4 rows of 5 blocks to make 4 borders. Add 2 borders to the sides of the quilt, then after adding a corner block to each end of each, add the top and bottom borders.

For Border 3 add in the same way as border 1.

ADDING BORDERS 4 – 6

Refer to the Border 4 – 6 assembly diagram for fabric placement. For Border 4 piece a total of 24 blocks as shown in the block assembly diagram using template HH triangles. Stitch into 4 rows of 6 blocks to make 4 borders. Add 2 borders to the sides of the quilt, then after adding a corner block to the ends of each, add the top and bottom borders.

For Border 5 add in the same way as border 1.

For Border 6 piece 4 borders as shown in the Border 4 – 6 assembly diagram, using the template JJ triangles for the main row, completing the border ends with template

KK and reverse KK triangles. Add 2 borders to the sides of the quilt, then after adding a corner block to the ends of each, add the top and bottom borders.

FINISHING THE QUILT

Press the quilt top. Seam the backing pieces using a ¼in (6mm) seam allowance to form a piece approx. 88in × 88in (223.5cm × 223.5cm). Layer the quilt top, batting and backing and baste together (see page 139). Using pastel thread for the light areas and blue/green for the darker areas stitch in the ditch along all the seams, then loosely stipple quilt across the surface of the quilt tracing the shapes of flowers where appropriate i.e. in the corner posts. Trim the quilt edges and attach the binding (see page 140).

Border 1 & 3 Assembly Diagram

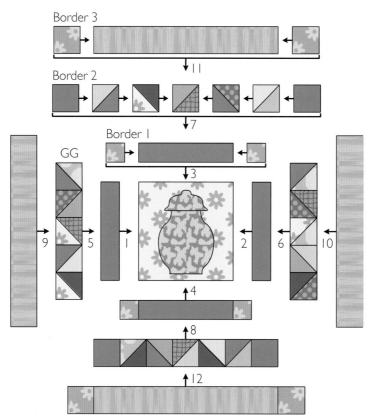

Border 4 & 6 Assembly Diagram

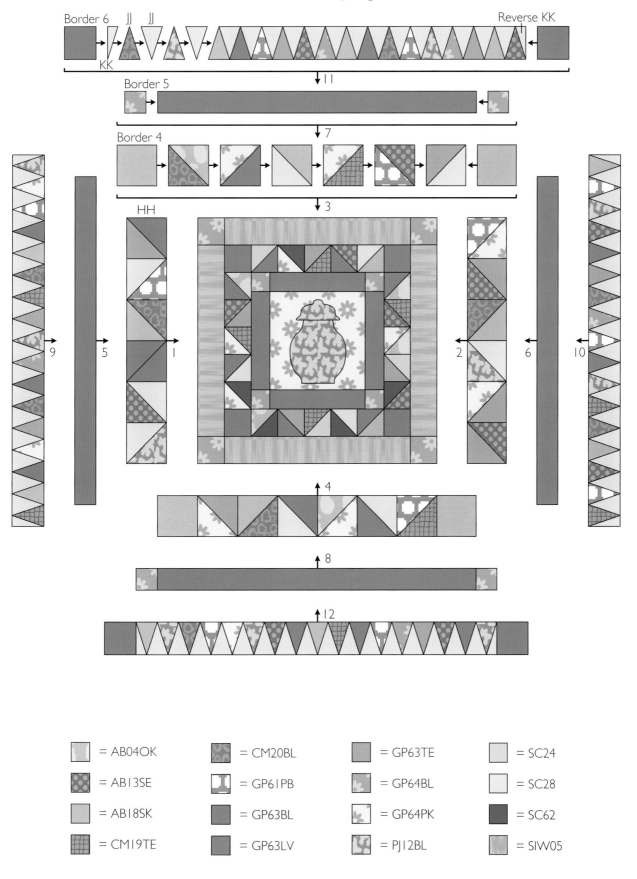

Border 6   JJ   JJ   Reverse KK

KK

Border 5

Border 4

HH

9   5   1   2   6   10

4

8

12

= AB04OK   = CM20BL   = GP63TE   = SC24

= AB13SE   = GP61PB   = GP64BL   = SC28

= AB18SK   = GP63BL   = GP64PK   = SC62

= CM19TE   = GP63LV   = PJ12BL   = SIW05

Octagons With Stars Quilt ★★

PAULINE SMITH

When the quilt top was pieced, Pauline decided the borders didn't quite work as she had wanted. The outer border looked too busy and dominated the understated quilt centre, which has mainly shot cottons and small pieces of restrained pattern. She decided to open up the borders by adding corner blocks. Everyone hates unpicking but in this case it was well worth the pain.

SIZE OF QUILT
The finished quilt will measure approx.
75in x 63in (190.5cm x 160cm).

MATERIALS
Patchwork Fabrics:
CHICKEN SCRATCH
Turquoise   CM05TQ: ¼yd (25cm)

FRECKLES
Cobalt   GP40CB: ⅜yd (35cm)
ISLANDS
Cobalt   GP49CB: ⅜yd (35cm)
SHIRT STRIPES
Midnight   GP51MD: ⅜yd (35cm)
Soft   GP51SF: ⅝yd (60cm)

WOVEN HAZE STRIPE
Blush   HZS09: ⅞yd (80cm)
Aegean   HZS20: ¼yd (25cm)
SHOT COTTON
Lavender   SC14: ¾yd (70cm)
Lilac   SC36: ½yd (45cm)
Jade   SC41: ⅜yd (35cm)

Aegean   SC46: ¼yd (25cm)
Forget–me–not   SC51: ⅜yd (35cm)
Brick   SC58: ⅜yd (35cm)
Clay   SC60: ⅜yd (35cm)

Inner Border:
SHOT COTTON
Forget–me–not   SC51: ½yd (45cm)

Outer Border:
SHIRT STRIPES
Soft   GP51SF: 1¼yds (1.2m)

Backing Fabric: 4yds (3.7m)
We suggest these fabrics for backing:
STARSHINE Blue, CM08BL
FRECKLES Cobalt, GP40CB
SHIRT STRIPES Soft, GP51SF

Binding:
WOVEN HAZE STRIPE
Aegean   HZS20: ⅝yd (60cm)

Batting:
83in × 71in (211cm × 180.5cm).

Quilting thread:
Toning hand or machine quilting thread.

Templates:

E   F   G   Reverse G   H

PATCH SHAPES
This pretty star block which finishes to 12in (30.5cm) is made using 1 square patch shape (Template E) and 3 triangle patch shapes (Templates F G & Reverse G and H). The blocks are straight set into simple rows and

the quilt is finished with a narrow inner border and a wider outer border, both with corner posts cut to size.

CUTTING OUT
Cut the fabric in the order stated, where appropriate reserve leftover strips and trim for later templates.
Template G & Reverse G: Cut 5⅜in (13.75cm) strips across the width of the fabric. Each strip will give you 30 patches per 45in (114cm) wide fabric. With the template right side up cut 32 in GP51SF, 15 in GP51MD, 12 in GP40CB, GP49CB and 9 in HZS20. Flip the template over, (right side down) for template Reverse G and cut 34 in GP51SF, 13 in GP51MD, 12 in GP40CB, GP49CB and 9 in HZS20. Tip: If you fold each strip in half lengthways and cut through both layers of the fabric at the same time you can cut the G and the Reverse G patch shapes at the same time.
Template F: Cut 4⅞in (12.5cm) strips across the width of the fabric. Each strip will give you 16 patches per 45in (114cm) wide fabric. Cut 21 in SC14, 16 in SC41, 15 in SC36, 9 in SC58, 8 in SC46, 7 in SC60 and 4 in SC51.
Template H: Fabric HZS09 ONLY: Cut 3½in (9cm) wide strips down the length of the fabric. This will ensure the correct stripe direction. Place the template with the long side along the cut strips and cut 80 template F triangles in HZS09.
Fabrics SC14, SC36, SC46, SC51, SC58 and SC60, cut 4⅞in (12.5cm) strips across the width of the fabric. Each strip will give you 16 patches per 45in (114cm) wide fabric. Cut 4⅞in (12.5cm) squares, then cut each square once diagonally to make 2 triangles, using the template as a guide. Cut 22 in SC14, 15 in

SC36, 12 in CM05TQ, SC51, 8 in SC58, 7 in SC60 and 4 in SC46.
Template E: Cut 4½in (11.5cm) strips across the width of the fabric, or trim strips from previous templates as appropriate. Each full strip will give you 9 patches per 45in (114cm) wide fabric. Cut 5 in GP49CB, 4 in GP51SF, 3 in HZS20, SC41, 2 in GP40CB, GP51MD and 1 in SC36.

Inner Border: Cut 6 strips 2½in (6.5cm) wide × width of fabric in SC51. Join as necessary and cut 2 strips 2½in × 60½in (6.5cm × 153.75cm) for the sides of the quilt and 2 strips 2½in × 48½in (6.5cm × 123.25cm) for the top and bottom of the quilt. Also cut 4 × 2½in (6.5cm) squares for the corner posts in SC58.

Outer Border: Cut 6 strips 6in (15.25cm) wide × width of fabric in GP51SF. Join as necessary and cut 2 strips 6in × 64½in (15.25cm × 163.75cm) for the sides of the quilt and 2 strips 6in × 52½in (15.25cm × 133.5cm) for the top and bottom of the quilt. Also cut 4 × 6in (15.25cm) squares for the corner posts in SC14.

Binding: Cut 7 strips 2½in (6.5cm) wide × width of fabric in HZS20.

Backing: Cut 2 pieces 44in × 71in (112cm × 180.5cm) in backing fabric.

MAKING THE BLOCKS
Use a ¼in (6mm) seam allowance throughout. Referring to the quilt assembly diagram for fabric placement piece 20 blocks. For each block piece 4 corner sections as shown in block assembly diagram a, then piece 4 star point sections as shown diagram

Block Assembly Diagrams

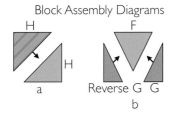

a

Reverse G   G

b

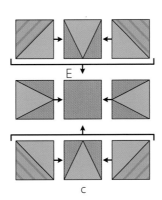

E

c

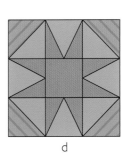

d

b. Assemble the block as shown in diagram c. The finished full block can be seen in diagram d.

MAKING THE QUILT

Join the blocks into 5 rows of 4 blocks then join the rows to form the quilt centre. Stitch the corner posts to the top and bottom inner and outer borders, then add the inner and outer borders to the quilt as indicated in the quilt assembly diagram.

FINISHING THE QUILT

Press the quilt top. Seam the backing pieces using a ¼in (6mm) seam allowance to form a piece approx. 83in x 71in (211cm x 180.5cm). Layer the quilt top, batting and backing and baste together (see page 139). Quilt in the ditch around the octagon shapes and around each star by hand or machine using toning quilting thread. Trim the quilt edges and attach the binding (see page 140).

Quilt Assembly Diagram

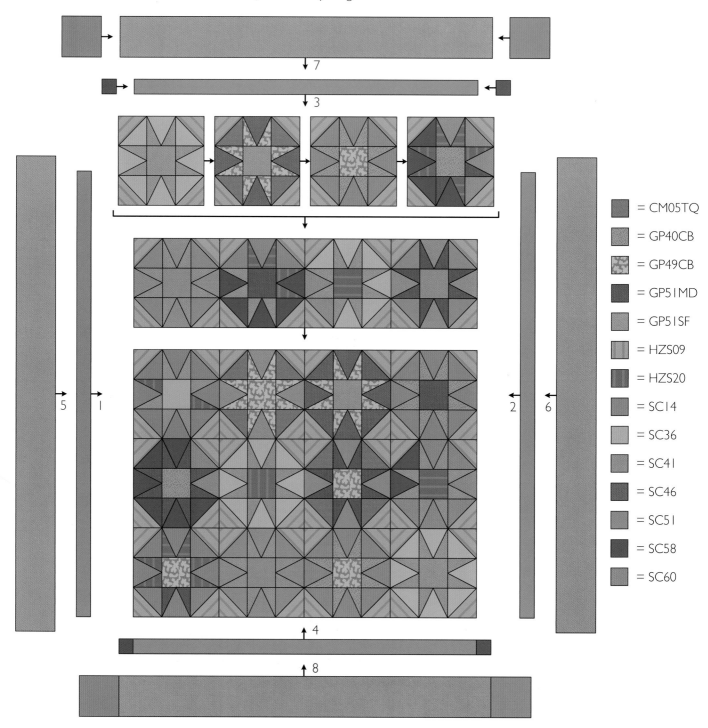

= CM05TQ
= GP40CB
= GP49CB
= GP51MD
= GP51SF
= HZS09
= HZS20
= SC14
= SC36
= SC41
= SC46
= SC51
= SC58
= SC60

Jane's Diamonds Pastel Quilt ★★★

KAFFE FASSETT

The soft, spring palette of this mirror imaged quilt is punctuated with a magenta French knot tied at the point of each diamond.

SIZE OF QUILT
The finished quilt will measure approx.
89in × 70⅜in (226cm × 178.75cm).

MATERIALS
Note: Some fabrics are 'fussy cut' to centre floral designs, extra fabric has been allows for this.

Patchwork Fabrics:
LILIES
Lime   GP45LM: ¾ yd (70cm)
ORGANIC DOTS
Contrast   GP53CO: ⅜ yd (35cm)
Spring   GP53SP: ¼ yd (25cm)
DAHLIA BLOOMS
Spring   GP54SP: ½ yd (45cm)
FLOATING FLOWERS
Pastel   GP56PT: ⅜ yd (35cm)
PAPER FANS
Cream   GP57CM: ½ yd (45cm)
SAMARKAND
Frost   GP58FR: ⅜ yd (35cm)
GUINEA FLOWER
Mauve   GP59MV: ¼ yd (25cm) or
use leftover from borders.
PAISLEY JUNGLE
Grey   GP60GY: ¼ yd (25cm)
Lime   GP60LM: ½ yd (45cm)
PANSY
Celadon   PJ01CD: ⅜ yd (35cm)
CORAL
Duckegg   PJ04DE: ⅜ yd (35cm)
GERANIUM LEAF
Lilac   PJ05LI: ¼ yd (25cm)
BANDED POPPY
Mint   PJ06MT: ⅜ yd (35cm)
SHOT COTTON
Blush   SC28: 3½ yds (3.2m)

Borders:
GUINEA FLOWER
Mauve   GP59MV: 2⅜ yds (2.2m)

Backing Fabric: 5½ yds (5m)
We suggest the following fabrics for backing:
GUINEA FLOWER Mauve, GP59MV
SAMARKAND Frost, GP58FR
DAHLIA BLOOMS Spring, GP54SP

Binding:
FLOATING FLOWERS
Pastel   GP56PT: ⅝ yd (60cm)

Batting:
97in × 78in (246.5cm × 198cm).

Quilting thread:
Approximately 7 skeins Anchor Soft Cotton shade 88 (magenta)

Toning machine quilting thread.

Templates:

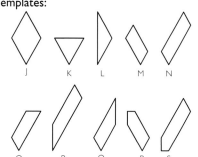

PATCH SHAPES
Based around a diamond patch shape (Template J) this quilt is sashed in a single fabric for a striking effect. There is also a large diamond shaped centre panel which is cut to size. The edges of the quilt are filled in using 2 triangle patch shapes (Templates K and L). Two main sashing strips are used (Templates M & Reverse M and N & Reverse N) with five further sashing strips (Templates O, P, Q, R & Reverse R and S) used to fill in along the quilt edges and corners.

Block Assembly Diagrams

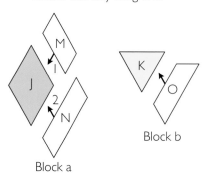

Block a

Block b

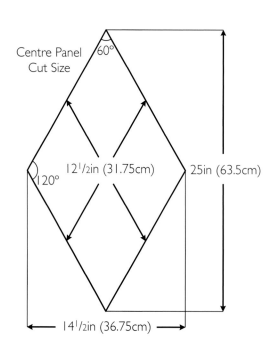

Centre Panel
Cut Size

60°

120°

12½in (31.75cm)   25in (63.5cm)

14½in (36.75cm)

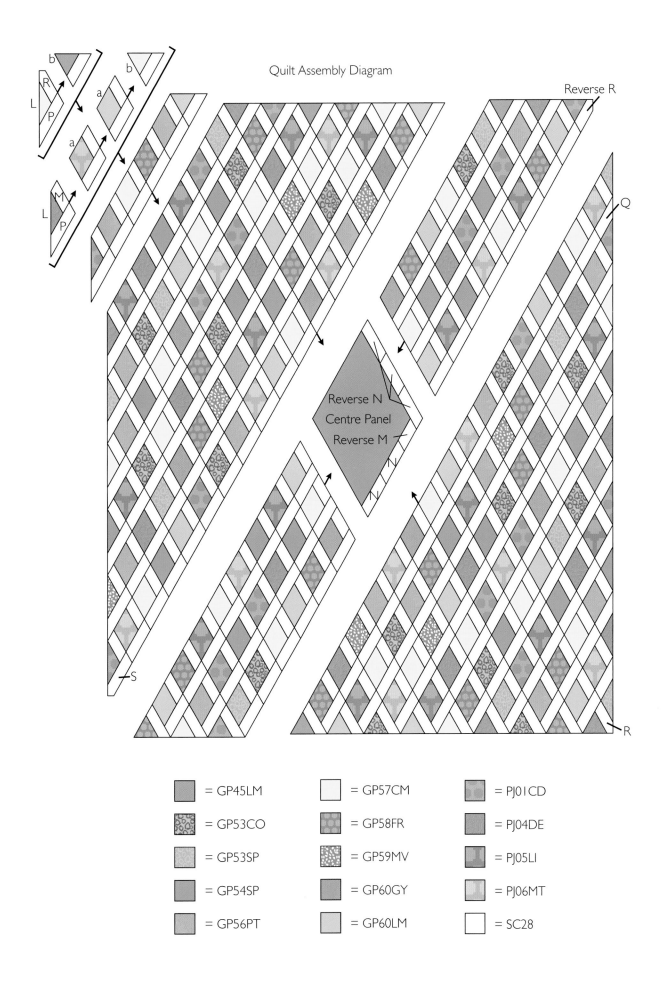

Quilt Assembly Diagram

	= GP45LM		= GP57CM		= PJ01CD
	= GP53CO		= GP58FR		= PJ04DE
	= GP53SP		= GP59MV		= PJ05LI
	= GP54SP		= GP60GY		= PJ06MT
	= GP56PT		= GP60LM		= SC28

Note: The fabric Kaffe chose for this sashing in this project is reversible, so you don't need to reverse templates M, N and R. However for the Jane's Diamonds Lapis version (see page 94) you will need to cut 'reverse' patches for these shapes.

CUTTING OUT

Cut the fabric in the order stated. Some fabrics are 'fussy cut', we suggest making a template from clear template plastic to allow easy centring of the designs.

Centre Panel: This is a large diamond which is fussy cut from GP45LI. We suggest making a paper template for this shape. The size is shown in the centre panel cut size diagram. You can check the angles are correct by using template J, as the centre panel is a scaled up version of template J.

Template J: Fussy cut template J patches centring the fabric designs for fabrics GP45LM, GP54SP, GP59MV, GP60GY, GP60LM and PJ06MT. Cut 16 in GP60LM, 14 in GP54SP, PJ06MT, 8 in GP60GY, 6 in GP59MV and 4 in GP45LM.

Other Fabrics: Cut 3½in (9cm) wide strips across the width of the fabric. Each strip will give you 9 patches per 45in (114cm) wide fabric. Cut 24 in GP57CM, 20 in GP56PT, 16 in GP58FR, PJ05LI, 14 in GP53CO, PJ04DE, 12 in PJ01CD and 8 in GP53SP.

Template K: Cut 3¾in (9.5cm) wide strips across the width of the fabric. Cut 4 in GP54SP, GP57CM, GP60LM, PJ04DE, 3 in GP58FR, PJ01CD and 2 in GP53CO. Reserve the remaining strip and trim for template L.

Template L: Cut 2¼in (5.75cm) wide strips across the width of the fabric. Cut 4 in PJ01CD, PJ04DE, 3 in GP53SP, GP54SP, GP57CM and 1 in GP59MV.

Template M: Cut 2in (5cm) wide strips across the width of the fabric. Each strip will give you 10 patches per 45in (114cm) wide fabric. Cut 195 in SC28.

Template N: Cut 2in (5cm) wide strips across the width of the fabric. Each strip will give you 7 patches per 45in (114cm) wide fabric. Cut 183 in SC28.

Template O: Cut 2in (5cm) wide strips across the width of the fabric. Each strip will give you 8 patches per 45in (114cm) wide fabric. Cut 22 in SC28.

Template P: Cut 2in (5cm) wide strips across the width of the fabric. Each strip will give you 5 patches per 45in (114cm) wide fabric. Cut 8 in SC28.

Template Q: Cut 2in (5cm) wide strips across the width of the fabric. Each strip will give you 6 patches per 45in (114cm) wide

fabric. Cut 8 in SC28.

Template R: Cut 2in (5cm) wide strips across the width of the fabric. Cut 3 in SC28.

Template S: Cut 2in (5cm) wide strips across the width of the fabric. Cut 1 in SC28.

Borders: From the length of the fabric cut 2 strips 4½in × 81½in (11.5cm × 207cm) and 2 strips 4½in × 70⅞in (11.5cm × 180cm) in GP59MV.

Binding: Cut 8 strips 2½in (6.5cm) wide × width of fabric in GP56PT.

Backing: Cut 2 pieces 39in × 97in (99cm × 246.5cm) in backing fabric.

MAKING THE BLOCKS

Using a ¼in (6mm) seam allowance throughout, piece the blocks as shown in the block assembly diagram referring to the quilt assembly diagram for fabric placement.

MAKING THE QUILT

Join sashing strips to the centre panel and lay out the pieced blocks as shown in the quilt assembly diagram completing the quilt edges as shown. Separate the diagonal rows and carefully stitch together. Join the rows to complete the quilt top. Finally add the borders in the order indicated in the border assembly diagram.

FINISHING THE QUILT

Press the quilt top. Seam the backing pieces using a ¼in (6mm) seam allowance to form a piece approx. 97in × 78in (246.5cm × 198cm). Layer the quilt top, batting and backing and baste together (see page 139). Using Anchor soft cotton shade 88, embroider French knots in all 4 corners of each diamond. Machine quilt the centre panel in the ditch and following the flowers and foliage. Trim the quilt edges and attach the binding (see page 140).

Border Assembly Diagram

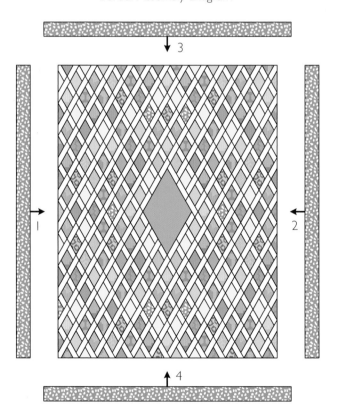

Jane's Diamonds Lapis Quilt ★★★
KAFFE FASSETT

The deep blue sashing gives this version of Jane's Diamonds the feeling of jewelled stained glass.

SIZE OF QUILT

The finished quilt will measure approx.
89in × 70⅜in (226cm × 178.75cm).

MATERIALS

Note: Some fabrics are 'fussy cut' to centre
floral designs, extra fabric has been allows for
this.

Patchwork Fabrics:

SHELLS
Fuchsia   CM13FU: ⅜yd (35cm)

CORAL FLOWERS
Royal   CM15RY: 3½yds (3.2m)
KIMONO
Cobalt/Turquoise   GP33CT: ¼yd (25cm)
LILIES
Malachite   GP45MA: ⅜yd (35cm)
Magenta   GP45MG: ½yd (45cm)
AURICULA
Indigo   GP52IN: ⅜yd (35cm)
DAHLIA BLOOMS
Cool   GP54CL: ½yd (45cm)

STRIPED VASE
Blue   GP55BL: ¼yd (25cm)
Grey   GP55GY: ¼yd (25cm)
FLOATING FLOWERS
Blue   GP56BL: ¼yd (25cm)
PAPER FANS
Green   GP57GN: ¼yd (25cm)
Teal   GP57TE: ⅜yd (35cm)
SAMARKAND
Purple   GP58PU: ⅜yd (35cm)
PAISLEY JUNGLE

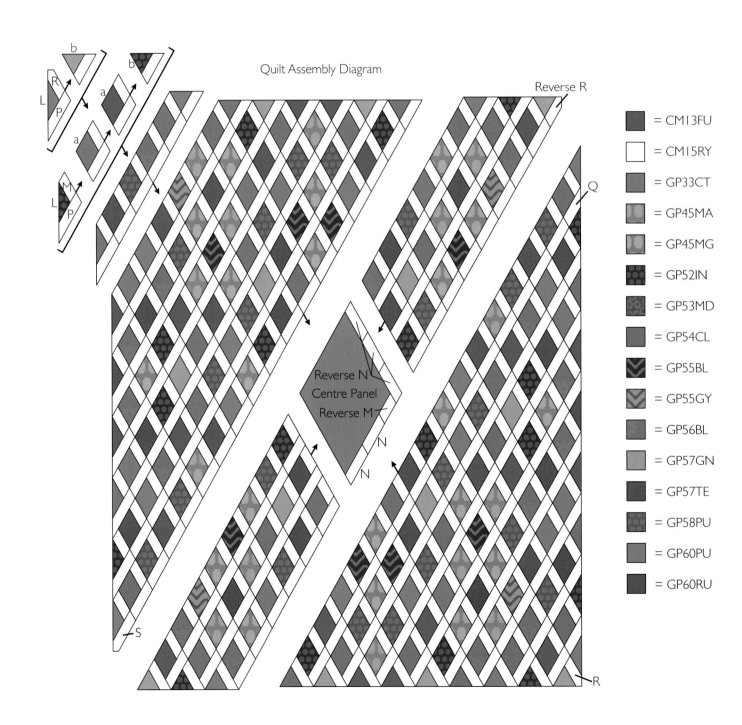

Quilt Assembly Diagram

= CM13FU
= CM15RY
= GP33CT
= GP45MA
= GP45MG
= GP52IN
= GP53MD
= GP54CL
= GP55BL
= GP55GY
= GP56BL
= GP57GN
= GP57TE
= GP58PU
= GP60PU
= GP60RU

Purple   GP60PU: ³⁄₈ yd (35cm)
Rust   GP60RU: ¹⁄₈ yd (15cm)

Borders:
ORGANIC DOTS
Midnight   GP53MD: 2³⁄₈ yds (2.2m)

Backing Fabric: 5½ yds (5m)
We suggest the following fabrics for backing:
CORAL FLOWERS Royal, CM15RY
STRIPED VASE Blue, GP55BL
FLOATING FLOWERS Blue, GP56BL

Binding:
FLOATING FLOWERS
Blue   GP56BL: ⁵⁄₈ yd (60cm)

Batting:
97in × 78in (246.5cm × 198cm).

Quilting thread:
Approximately 7 skeins Anchor Soft Cotton
shade 239 (green)
Toning machine quilting thread.

Templates:
See Jane's Diamonds Pastel Quilt.

PATCH SHAPES
See Jane's Diamonds Pastel Quilt Instructions.
Note: The fabric Kaffe chose for this sashing
in this project is NOT reversible, so you will
need to reverse templates M, N and R.

CUTTING OUT
Cut the fabric in the order stated. Some
fabrics are 'fussy cut', we suggest making a
template from clear template plastic to allow
easy centring of the designs.
Centre Panel: This is a large diamond which
is cut from GP60PU (the fabric was not
'fussy cut' for this version). We suggest
making a paper template for this shape. The
size is shown in the Jane's Diamonds Pastel
Quilt centre panel cut size diagram. You can
check the angles are correct by using
template J, as the centre panel is a scaled up
version of template J.
Template J: Fussy cut template J patches
centring the fabric designs for fabrics
GP33CT, GP45MA, GP45MG, GP54CL,
GP55BL and GP55GY. Cut 24 in GP54CL, 20
in GP45MG, 14 in GP45MA, 8 in GP33CT,
GP55BL and 4 in GP55GY.
Other Fabrics: Cut 3½ in (9cm) wide strips
across the width of the fabric. Each strip will
give you 9 patches per 45in (114cm) wide
fabric. Cut 22 in GP58PU, 20 in GP57TE, 16
in GP56BL, 12 in CM13FU, GP52IN,

GP60PU, 8 in GP60RU and 6 in GP57GN.
Reserve the remaining strip and trim for
template L where appropriate.
Template K: Cut 3¾ in (9.5cm) wide strips
across the width of the fabric. Cut 8 in
GP57GN, 4 in CM13FU, GP52IN, GP54CL
and GP60PU. Reserve the remaining strip
and trim for template L.
Template L: Cut 2¼ in (5.75cm) wide strips
across the width of the fabric. Cut 4 in
CM13FU, GP52IN, GP54CL, GP60PU and 2
in GP57TE.
Template M & Reverse M: Cut 2in (5cm)
wide strips across the width of the fabric.
Each strip will give you 10 patches per 45in
(114cm) wide fabric. Cut 194 in CM15RY,
reverse the template and cut 1 in CM15RY.
Template N: Cut 2in (5cm) wide strips
across the width of the fabric. Each strip will
give you 7 patches per 45in (114cm) wide
fabric. Cut 180 in CM15RY, reverse the
template and cut 3 in CM15RY.
Template O: Cut 2in (5cm) wide strips
across the width of the fabric. Each strip will
give you 8 patches per 45in (114cm) wide
fabric. Cut 22 in CM15RY.
Template P: Cut 2in (5cm) wide strips across
the width of the fabric. Each strip will give
you 5 patches per 45in (114cm) wide fabric.
Cut 8 in CM15RY.
Template Q: Cut 2in (5cm) wide strips

across the width of the fabric. Each strip will
give you 6 patches per 45in (114cm) wide
fabric. Cut 8 in CM15RY.
Template R: Cut 2in (5cm) wide strips across
the width of the fabric. Cut 2 in CM15RY,
reverse the template and cut 1 in CM15RY.
Template S: Cut 2in (5cm) wide strips across
the width of the fabric. Cut 1 in CM15RY.

Borders: From the length of the fabric cut 2
strips 4½ in × 81½ in (11.5cm × 207cm) and 2
strips 4½ in × 70⅞ in (11.5cm × 180cm) in
GP53MD.

Binding: Cut 8 strips 2½ in (6.5cm) wide ×
width of fabric in GP56BL.

Backing: Cut 2 pieces 39in × 97in (99cm ×
246.5cm) in backing fabric.

MAKING THE BLOCKS
See Jane's Diamonds Pastel Quilt Instructions.

MAKING THE QUILT
See Jane's Diamonds Pastel Quilt Instructions.
Note: The reverse template shapes M and N
are used around the centre panel.

FINISHING THE QUILT
See Jane's Diamonds Pastel Quilt Instructions.
Note: Use Anchor soft cotton shade 239 for
the French knots in this version.

Border Assembly Diagram

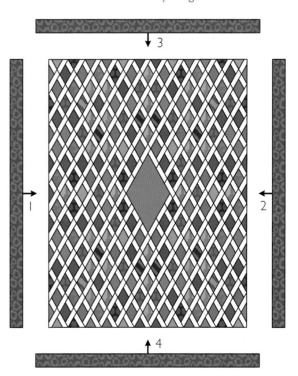

Pauline's Promise Quilt ★★★

REBEKAH LYNCH

Some fabrics plead to be featured. Kaffe's Flower Baskets in magenta is a perfect example. Teamed with other Kaffe Fassett fabrics in saturated colours from the Rowan collection and simple piecing, this quilt indeed fulfils my 'promise to Pauline'.

SIZE OF QUILT
The finished quilt will measure approx. 71in × 88in (180.25cm × 223.5cm).

MATERIALS
Patchwork Fabrics:
LOTUS LEAF
Red   GP29RD: ½yd (45cm)

Wine	GP29WN: ¼yd (25cm)	
LEAVES		
Red	GP30RD: ¼yd (25cm)	
ZINNIA		
Lime	GP31LM: ¼yd (25cm)	
Magenta	GP31MG: ¼yd (25cm)	
KIMONO		
Crimson/Magenta	GP33CM: ½yd (45cm)	

SPOOLS
Magenta   GP34MG: ¼yd (25cm)
ROMANY
Red   GP39RD: 1¾yds (1.6m)
                       includes binding.
PLANETS
Rose   GP41RO: ½yd (45cm)
EMBROIDERED LEAF

Violet	GP42VI:	¼yd (25cm)
PUFF		
Red	GP43RD:	¼yd (25cm)
LILIES		
Orange	GP45OR:	¼yd (25cm)
CLOISONNE		
Magenta	GP46MG:	½yd (45cm)
Terracotta	GP46TC:	¼yd (25cm)
BURNT WOOD ROSE		
Wine	GP47WN:	¼yd (25cm)
FLOWER BASKET		
Duck Egg	GP48DE:	¼yd (25cm)
Magenta	GP48MG:	3¼yds (3m)
Pink	GP48PK:	¼yd (25cm)
ISLANDS		
Pink	GP49PK:	¼yd (25cm)
DAHLIA BLOOMS		
Lush	GP54LS:	¼yd (25cm)
STRIPED VASE		
Red	GP55RD:	½yd (45cm)
FLOATING FLOWERS		
Yellow	GP56YE:	¼yd (25cm)
PAPER FANS		
Red	GP57RD:	¼yd (25cm)
GUINEA FLOWER		
Pink	GP59PK:	¼yd (25cm)
PAISLEY JUNGLE		
Green	GP60GN:	¼yd (25cm)
Rust	GP60RU:	¼yd (25cm)
Tangerine	GP60TN:	¼yd (25cm)
VEGETABLE LEAVES		
Wine	MN05WN:	¼yd (25cm)

Backing Fabric: 5½yds (5m)
We suggest these fabrics for backing:
CLOISONNE Terracotta, GP46TC
BURNT WOOD ROSE Wine, GP47WN
DAHLIA BLOOMS Lush, GP54LS

Binding:
ROMANY
Red   GP39RD:
                       See patchwork fabrics.

Batting:
79in × 96in (200.5cm × 244cm).

Quilting thread:
Toning machine quilting thread.

Templates:

EE   NN

PATCH SHAPES
Freeform long cabin blocks are set 'on point'
alternated with fussy cut squares of Flower

basket fabric, cut to size, which are each
framed with sashing strips, also cut to size.
The edges of the quilt are completed with 2
triangular pieced blocks which both use 1
square patch shape (Template EE) and 1
triangle patch shape (Template NN). Each of
the triangular pieced blocks has sashing strips
on the 2 short sides, these are cut to size.
The quilt is finished with a simple border.

CUTTING OUT
To reduce waste we suggest drawing round
the templates onto the reverse of the fabrics
for the best fit before cutting. This will leave
the remaining fabrics available for the log
cabin strips.

Alternate Block Squares: Fussy cut a total of
12 × 10½in (26.75cm) squares in GP48MG.
The 4 squares for the centre vertical row are
cut 'on point' centred on the flower basket
design in the fabric, for these the flower
baskets look upright. The side rows are cut
'straight' so that when they are set in the
quilt the baskets are tilted. Check the
photograph for more information. The
leftover fabric is used in the log cabin blocks.
Alternate Block Sashing Strips: Cut 24 strips
1½in × 12½in (3.75cm × 31.75cm) and 24
strips 1½in × 10½in (3.75cm × 26.75cm) in
GP39RD.
Template EE: (Used for log cabin centres and
setting blocks). Cut 3in (7.75cm) squares. Cut

Log Cabin Block

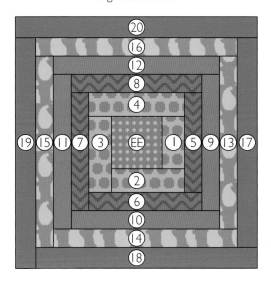

Alternate Block

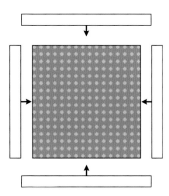

Side Setting Block

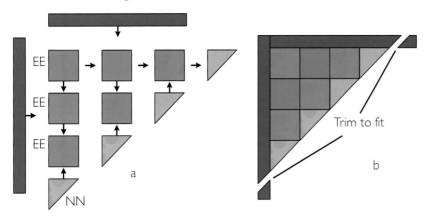

EE EE EE NN

a

Trim to fit

b

Corner Setting Block

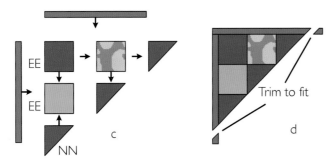

EE EE NN

c

Trim to fit

d

be trimmed to fit exactly later.

Binding: Cut 8 strips 2½in (6.5cm) wide × width of fabric in GP39RD.

Backing: Cut 2 pieces 40in × 96in (101.5cm × 244cm) in backing fabric.

MAKING THE BLOCKS

Use a ¼in (6mm) seam allowance throughout. Referring to the quilt assembly diagram for fabric placement piece 20 log cabin blocks. The 'logs' are added to the block centre (template EE squares) as shown in the log cabin diagram and trimmed to fit as you go. Use a single fabric for each round of 'logs'. Aim for the blocks to be about 13in (33cm) square. Then trim to exactly 12½in (31.75cm) square. Some of Rebekah's blocks ended up with only 16 logs as the strips on these blocks were wider.

Add sashing strips to the fussy cut GP48MG squares to make alternate blocks as shown in the alternate block diagram. Make 12.

The side setting blocks are pieced from 6 template EE squares and 4 template NN triangles as shown in side setting block diagram a. Add sashing strips to the 2 short sides on the block as shown, then trim the sashing to fit (see side setting block diagram b).

The corner setting blocks are pieced from 3 template EE squares and 3 template NN triangles as shown in corner setting block diagram c. Add sashing strips to the 2 short sides on the block as shown, then trim the sashing to fit (see corner setting block diagram d).

MAKING THE QUILT

Lay out all the log cabin blocks and alternate blocks in diagonal rows, fill in the edges with the side setting blocks and the corners with the corner setting blocks, as shown in the quilt assembly diagram. Carefully separate into diagonal rows and join. Finally trim the top and bottom borders to fit and join to the quilt centre, then trim the side borders and join to the quilt centre.

FINISHING THE QUILT

Press the quilt top. Seam the backing pieces using a ¼in (6mm) seam allowance to form a piece approx. 79in × 96in (200.5cm × 244cm). Layer the quilt top, batting and backing and baste together (see page 139). Using toning machine quilting thread, free motion quilt in a meandering pattern across the surface of the quilt. Trim the quilt edges and attach the binding (see page 140).

11 in GP33CM, GP46MG, 9 in GP31MG, 8 in GP42VI, GP43RD, GP47WN, 7 in GP45OR, 6 in GP29RD, GP41RO, GP60GN, 5 in GP39RD, 4 in GP34MG, GP59PK, GP60RU, MN05WN, 3 in GP60TN, 2 in GP29WN, GP30RD, GP48MG, GP55RD, GP56YE, 1 in GP54LS and GP57RD.

Template NN: The straight grain must run along the long side of the triangles, this will prevent the quilt sides from being on the bias and stretchy. Cut 16 in GP46MG, 8 in GP34MG, GP47WN, GP60RU, MN05WN, 6 in GP29WN, GP55RD, 4 in GP45OR and GP60TN.

Side Block Sashing Strips: Cut a total of 14 strips 1½in × 13in (3.75cm × 33cm), 4 in GP57RD, 2 in GP29WN, GP42VI, GP46MG, GP54LS and GP55RD. Cut a total of 14 strips 1½in × 12in (3.75cm × 30.5cm), 4 in GP57RD, 2 in GP29WN, GP42VI, GP46MG,

GP54LS and GP55RD. These are cut oversize and will be trimmed later.

Corner Block Sashing Strips: Cut a total of 4 strips 1in × 9½in (2.5cm × 24.25cm), 2 in GP54LS and 2 in MN05WN. Cut a total of 4 strips 1in × 9in (2.5cm × 23cm), 2 in GP54LS and 2 in MN05WN. These are cut oversize and will be trimmed later.

Log Cabin Blocks: From the remaining fabrics cut strips for the log cabin blocks. The width of these strips can vary from 1⅜in to 2in (3.5cm to 5cm). We suggest cutting strips and piecing as you go for these blocks.

Border: Cut 8 strips 2in (5cm) wide × width of fabric in GP39RD. Join as necessary and cut 2 strips 2in × 86in (5cm × 218.6cm) for the sides of the quilt and 2 strips 2in × 72in (5cm × 182.75cm) for the top and bottom of the quilt. These are a little oversized and will

Quilt Assembly Diagram

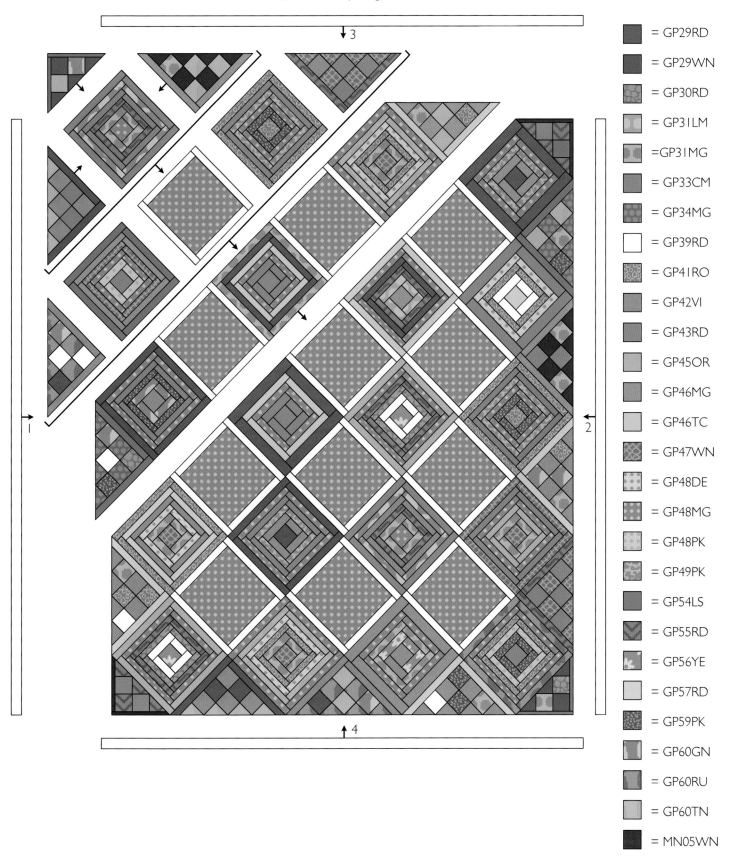

= GP29RD
= GP29WN
= GP30RD
= GP31LM
=GP31MG
= GP33CM
= GP34MG
= GP39RD
= GP41RO
= GP42VI
= GP43RD
= GP45OR
= GP46MG
= GP46TC
= GP47WN
= GP48DE
= GP48MG
= GP48PK
= GP49PK
= GP54LS
= GP55RD
= GP56YE
= GP57RD
= GP59PK
= GP60GN
= GP60RU
= GP60TN
= MN05WN

Forget–Me–Not Cabins Quilt ★★

BETSY MENEFEE RICKLES

The brilliant colours of our shot cottons are the perfect venue for creating the intuitive, free–style log cabin blocks in Betsy's quilt. The inspiration for Betsy's design was a group of hand-pieced blocks that she pieced while touring Italy. All she took were the fabric, needle, thread and scissors and, once on her way, she cut small squares and strips, sewing them together using the 'stitch and flip' method in a relaxed style.

SIZE OF QUILT
The finished quilt will measure approx.
48in × 48in (122cm × 122cm).

MATERIALS
SHOT COTTON
Ginger	SC01: ⅛yd (15cm)
Chartreuse	SC12: scraps
Rosy	SC32: ⅛yd (15cm)
Watermelon	SC33: scraps
Sunshine	SC35: ¾ yd (70cm)
Lilac	SC36: scraps
Apple	SC39: ⅛yd (15cm)
Jade	SC41: ⅜yd (35cm)
Lime	SC43: ¾yd (70cm)
Scarlet	SC44: ⅛yd (15cm)
Aegean	SC46: ⅛yd (15cm)
Grape	SC47: ⅛yd (15cm)
Forget–me–not	SC51: ⅜yd (35cm)

Backing Fabric:
The backing for this quilt was pieced from strips and rectangles of some of the Shot Cottons used in the quilt. We suggest choosing 5 of your favourite colours and buying an extra ½yd (45cm) of each. This will give you plenty to piece a backing. Alternatively use 2⅜yds (2.15m) of any one of the fabrics.

Batting:
54in × 54in (137cm × 137cm).

Quilting thread:
Toning machine quilting thread.

PATCH SHAPES
The theory behind a log cabin block, to create a piece by building around a central square, lends itself to whimsical piecing. The goal of this quilt is to create your log cabin blocks with strip after strip, not worrying about measuring but proceeding with what satisfies your eye until you reach the desired block size. In this case Betsy was aiming towards a 9in (23cm) square block size, which was then trimmed to 8½in (21.5cm) square (finishes to 8in (20.25cm). The blocks were then sashed and surrounded with multiple borders, added in the same whimsical way as the original blocks.

CUTTING OUT
Blocks: Cut a selection of strips across the width from all the fabrics, about 1in to 2in (2.5cm to 5cm) wide. As you create and add to your blocks you can trim as you go, adding in the odd wider and narrower strip to suit. The finished strips vary from ¼ to 3inches

(6mm to 7.5cm).

Sashing: Cut 12 strips 8½in × 1½in (21.5cm × 3.75cm) for the vertical sashing and 4 strips 28½in × 1½in for the horizontal sashing in SC35.

Borders: Cut a selection of strips across the width of the fabric. The borders vary from 1½in to 4½in (3.75cm to 11.5cm). The outer borders are pieced.

Backing: If using a single fabric for backing cut 1 piece 42in × 54in (107cm × 137cm), 1 piece 42in × 13in (107cm × 33cm) and 1 piece 13in × 13in (33cm × 33cm) in backing fabric.

MAKING AND SASHING THE BLOCKS
Use a ¼in (6mm) seam allowance throughout. Refer to the quilt centre assembly diagram for guidance with fabric placement. First take a block centre square or rectangle, see block assembly diagram a. Then choose a second fabric and stitch to one side of the centre as shown in diagram b, flip open and trim to fit. Always press the seam allowances away from the block centre. The next 'log' is 'sub–pieced' using the same stitch

Block Assembly Diagrams

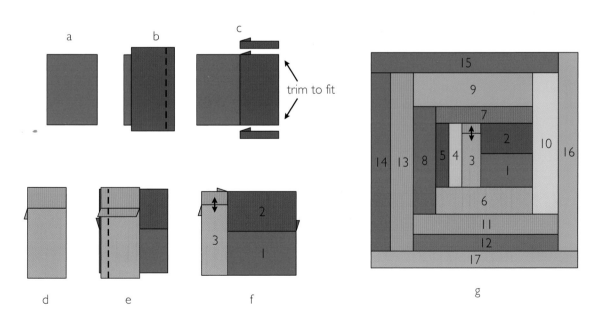

and flip method from 2 fabrics as shown in diagram d. Add this 'log' to the centre section (see diagram e), flip open and trim to fit as before (see diagram f).

In traditional log cabin the block is rotated 90 degrees for each new log to be added, however in this whimsical free–style method Betsy added logs in any order to create her very individual blocks. Diagram g shows a complete block, the numbers indicate the order in which the logs were added for this block. Carry on adding logs to the block in the same manner until it measures about 9in (23cm) square. Trim to 8½in (21.5cm) square. Make 9 blocks.

Join the blocks into 3 rows of 3 blocks, interspacing with the vertical sashing strips. Join the rows interspacing with the horizontal sashing strips, as shown in the quilt centre assembly diagram.

ADDING THE BORDERS
The first border is added as shown in the

Quilt Centre Assembly Diagram

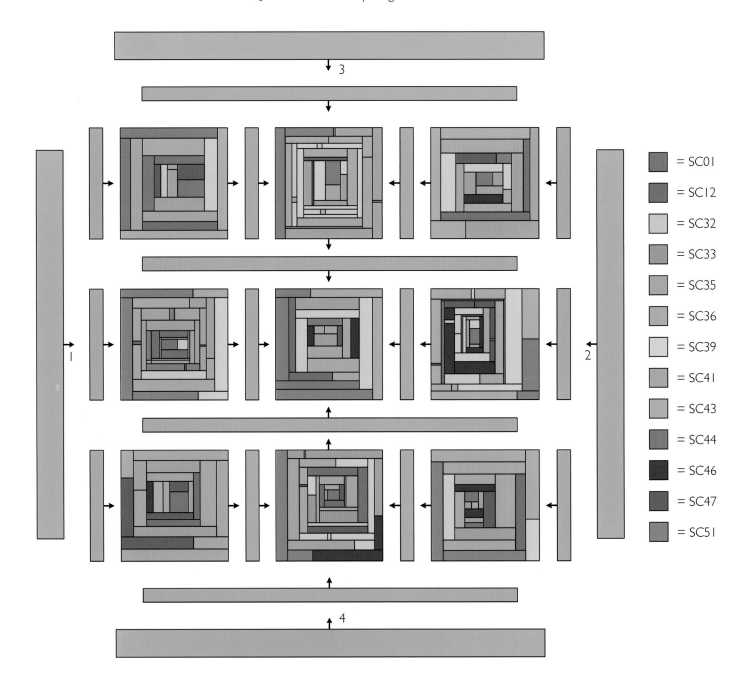

= SC01
= SC12
= SC32
= SC33
= SC35
= SC36
= SC39
= SC41
= SC43
= SC44
= SC46
= SC47
= SC51

quilt centre assembly diagram. After that, other strips are added in a similar way to the blocks in a whimsical order. The quilt border assembly diagram shows the order in which Betsy added her borders. The final outer borders were 'sub–pieced' to incorporate a flash of contrasting fabric before being added to the quilt.

FINISHING THE QUILT

Press the quilt top. If using a single fabric seam the backing pieces using a ¼in (6mm) seam allowance to form a piece approx 54in x 54in (137cm x 137cm), if piecing a backing make a backing the same size. Layer the quilt top, batting and backing and baste together (see page 139). Using toning machine quilting thread quilt in the

ditch in the block and border seams. Betsy added some additional quilting lines to the SC35 sashing and borders. Trim the quilt edges evenly. Peel the quilt front and backing back from the batting and trim the edge of the batting back by ⅜in (1cm) Turn the quilt front and backing edges in by ¼in (6mm) and slipstitch the quilt to the backing.

Quilt Border Assembly Diagram

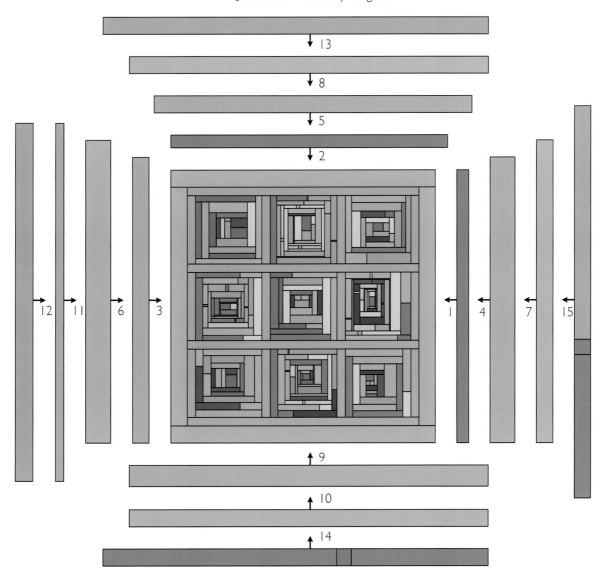

Tropical Frothy Quilt ★

LIZA PRIOR LUCY

When I saw Amy's first fabric collection designed for Rowan, I knew I wanted to do large pieces so the boldness of her fabrics would be shown to its greatest advantage. I prefer low contrast quilts, so I selected only her mid-range colours to do this version of Frothy. I think it lives up to its name, only this time it is a "frothy" fruit salad.

SIZE OF QUILT
The finished quilt will measure approx. 78in x 65in (198cm x 165cm).

MATERIALS
Patchwork Fabrics:
EYE LASHES
Orange   AB01OR: ¼yd (25cm)

SEEDS
Duck Egg   AB03DE: ¼yd (25cm)
Okra   AB03OK: ¼yd (25cm)
HENNA PAISLEY
Blue   AB04BL: ¼yd (25cm)
Pink   AB04PK: ½yd (45cm)
ROYAL GARDEN
Turquoise   AB06TQ: ¼yd (25cm)

CORIANDER
Blue   AB07BL: ¼yd (25cm)
Clay   AB07CY: ¼yd (25cm)
Olive   AB07OV: ¼yd (25cm)
Pink   AB07PK: ½yd (45cm)
Sea Green   AB07SG: ¼yd (25cm)
ACANTHUS
Duck Egg   AB08DE: ¼yd (25cm)

| Teal | AB08TE: ¼yd (25cm) |

CHRYSANTHEMUM

Blue	AB10BL: ¼yd (25cm)
Mustard	AB10MU: ½yd (45cm)
Okra	AB10OK: ¼yd (25cm)
Orange	AB10OR: ¼yd (25cm)
Olive	AB10OV: ¼yd (25cm)

Border:

OXFORD STRIPE

| Lime | AB05LM: 1¼yds (1.15m) |

SHOT COTTON

| Apple | SC39: ⅝yd (60cm) |

Backing Fabric: 4⅛yds (3.8m)
We suggest these fabrics for backing:
KASHMIR Okra, AB11OK
CHRYSANTHEMUM Okra, AB10OK
CORIANDER Blue, AB07BL

Binding:

SEEDS

Okra   AB03OK: ⅝yd (60cm)

Batting:
86in × 73in (218.5cm × 185.5cm).

Quilting thread:
Soft olive green machine quilting thread.

Templates:

T   U

PATCH SHAPES
The blocks in this quilt, which finish to 13in (33cm), are pieced using a triangle patch shape (Template T). The blocks are straight set into simple rows and the quilt is finished with a pieced border which uses the main triangle patch shape (Template T) and an additional larger triangle patch shape (Template U). You will find half template U on page 129. Take a large piece of paper, fold, place the edge of template U to the fold of paper, trace around shape and cut out. Open out for the complete template.

CUTTING OUT
Template T: Cut 7⅜in (18.75cm) strips across the width of the fabric. Each strip will give you 10 patches per 45in (114cm) wide fabric. Cut 7⅜in (18.75cm) squares, cut each square diagonally to form 2 triangles using the template as a guide. Cut 11 in AB04PK, AB07PK, AB10MU, 10 in AB06TQ, AB07CY, 9

in AB03OK, AB04BL, AB10OK, 8 in AB01OR, AB03DE, AB07BL, AB07OV, AB07SG, AB08DE, AB08TE, AB10BL, AB10OR and AB10OV.

Border

Template T: Cut 7⅜in (18.75cm) strips across the width of the fabric. Each strip will give you 10 patches per 45in (114cm) wide fabric. Cut 7⅜in (18.75cm) squares, cut each square diagonally to form 2 triangles using the template as a guide. Important: Refer to the quilt assembly diagram for stripe direction before you cut the squares diagonally. Cut 16 in AB05LM.

Template U: Cut 7⅛in (18cm) wide strips across the width of the fabric. Each strip will give you 5 patches per 45in (114cm) wide fabric. Place the template with the long side along the cut edge of the strip, this will ensure the long side of the triangles will not have a bias edge. Cut 18 in SC39 and 14 in AB05LM.

Binding: Cut 8 strips 2½in (6.5cm) wide × width of fabric in AB03OK.

Backing: Cut 2 pieces 44in × 73in (112cm × 185.5cm) in backing fabric.

MAKING THE BLOCKS
Use a ¼in (6mm) seam allowance throughout. Referring to the quilt assembly diagram for fabric placement piece 20 blocks as shown in block assembly diagrams a and b.

MAKING THE QUILT
Join the blocks into 5 rows of 4 blocks then join the rows to form the quilt centre. Piece the borders and add to the quilt as indicated in the quilt assembly diagram.

FINISHING THE QUILT
Press the quilt top. Seam the backing pieces using a ¼in (6mm) seam allowance to form a piece approx. 86in × 73in (218.5cm × 185.5cm). Layer the quilt top, batting and backing and baste together (see page 139). Using soft olive green machine quilting thread quilt in a loose meandering pattern across the surface of the quilt centre. You can incorporate floral themes to add interest. In the SC39 triangles free motion quilt flowers and foliage to fill the shape, or loosely stipple quilt if you prefer. Quilt parallel lines 1½in (3.75cm) apart following the seam lines in the AB05LM border triangles. See the detail photograph on page 12. Trim the quilt edges and attach the binding (see page 140).

Block Assembly Diagrams

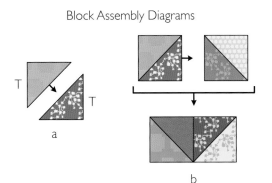

a

b

Quilt Assembly Diagram

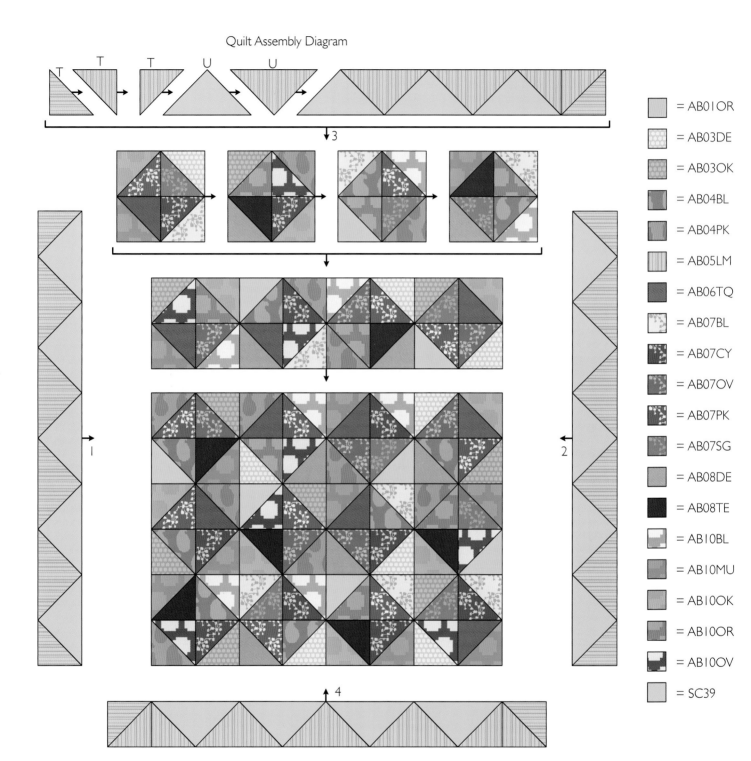

= AB01OR

= AB03DE

= AB03OK

= AB04BL

= AB04PK

= AB05LM

= AB06TQ

= AB07BL

= AB07CY

= AB07OV

= AB07PK

= AB07SG

= AB08DE

= AB08TE

= AB10BL

= AB10MU

= AB10OK

= AB10OR

= AB10OV

= SC39

Blue and White Frothy Quilt ★

KAFFE FASSETT

This wonderfully simple to construct quilt really shows off my new collection of prints. I like the way enormous florals give an 'airy clouds in the sky' feel to the denser, more monotone prints.

SIZE OF QUILT
The finished quilt will measure approx. 78in x 65in (198cm x 165cm).

MATERIALS
Patchwork Fabrics (includes Borders):
WALL FLOWERS
Pink	AB17PK: ¼yd (25cm)	

TREE PEONY
Ivory	AB18IV: ¼yd (25cm)
Pink	AB18PK: ½yd (45cm)
Sky Blue	AB18SK: ½yd (45cm)

MUMS
Blue	CM20BL: ¼yd (25cm)

VERBENA
Powder Blue	GP61PB: ¼yd (25cm)
Pink	GP61PK: ¼yd (25cm)

MINTON
Blue	GP63BL: ¼yd (25cm)
Lavender	GP63LV: ¼yd (25cm)

POTENTILLA
Lavender	GP64LV: 1¼yds (1.15m)
Pink	GP64PK: ¼yd (25cm)

GERANIUM
Duck Egg	PJ07DE: ¼yd (25cm)

MORNING GLORY
Blue	PJ08BL: ¼yd (25cm)
Pink	PJ08PK: ¼yd (25cm)

HOLLYHOCKS
Blue	PJ09BL: ¼yd (25cm)

FOXGLOVES
Blue	PJ10BL: ¼yd (25cm)
Pastel	PJ10PT: ¼yd (25cm)

LUSCIOUS
Pink	PJ11PK: ½yd (45cm)
Spring	PJ11SP: ¼yd (25cm)

CORAL LEAF
Blue	PJ12BL: 1¼yds (1.15m)

Backing Fabric: 4⅛yds (3.8m)
We suggest these fabrics for backing:
KIMONO Lavender Blue, GP33LB
PAISLEY JUNGLE Grey, GP60GY

Binding:
MUMS
Blue	CM20BL: ⅝yd (60cm)

Batting:
86in x 73in (218.5cm x 185.5cm).

Quilting thread:
Machine quilting thread in mauve.

Templates:
See Tropical Frothy Quilt.

PATCH SHAPES
See Tropical Frothy Quilt.

CUTTING OUT
Template T: Cut 7⅜in (18.75cm) strips across the width of the fabric. Each strip will give you 10 patches per 45in (114cm) wide fabric. Cut 7⅜in (18.75cm) squares, cut each square diagonally to form 2 triangles using the template as a guide. Cut 13 in AB18PK, 12 in AB18SK, PJ11PK, 10 in CM20BL, GP61PB, GP61PK, GP63BL, PJ09BL, 8 in AB17PK, GP63LV, PJ10BL, PJ10PT, 7 in AB18IV, GP64PK, PJ08PK, 6 in PJ08BL, PJ12BL, 4 in PJ07DE and PJ11SP.

Border
Template T: Cut 7⅜in (18.75cm) strips across the width of the fabric. Each strip will give you 10 patches per 45in (114cm) wide fabric. Cut 7⅜in (18.75cm) squares, cut each square diagonally to form 2 triangles using the template as a guide. Cut 16 in GP64LV.
Template U: Cut 7⅛in (18cm) wide strips across the width of the fabric. Each strip will give you 5 patches per 45in (114cm) wide fabric. Place the template with the long side along the cut edge of the strip, this will ensure the long side of the triangles will not have a bias edge. Cut 18 in PJ12BL and 14 in GP64LV.

Binding: Cut 8 strips 2½in (6.5cm) wide x width of fabric in CM20BL.

Backing: Cut 2 pieces 44in x 73in (112cm x 185.5cm) in backing fabric.

MAKING THE BLOCKS
See Tropical Frothy Quilt instructions.

MAKING THE QUILT
See Tropical Frothy Quilt instructions.

FINISHING THE QUILT
Press the quilt top. Seam the backing pieces using a ¼in (6mm) seam allowance to form a piece approx. 86in x 73in (218.5cm x 185.5cm). Layer the quilt top, batting and backing and baste together (see page 139). Using toning mauve machine quilting thread, quilt in a loose meandering pattern across the surface of the quilt. You can incorporate floral themes to add interest. Quilt parallel lines 1½in (3.75cm) apart following the seam lines in the GP64LV and GP63BL border triangles. Trim the quilt edges and attach the binding (see page 140).

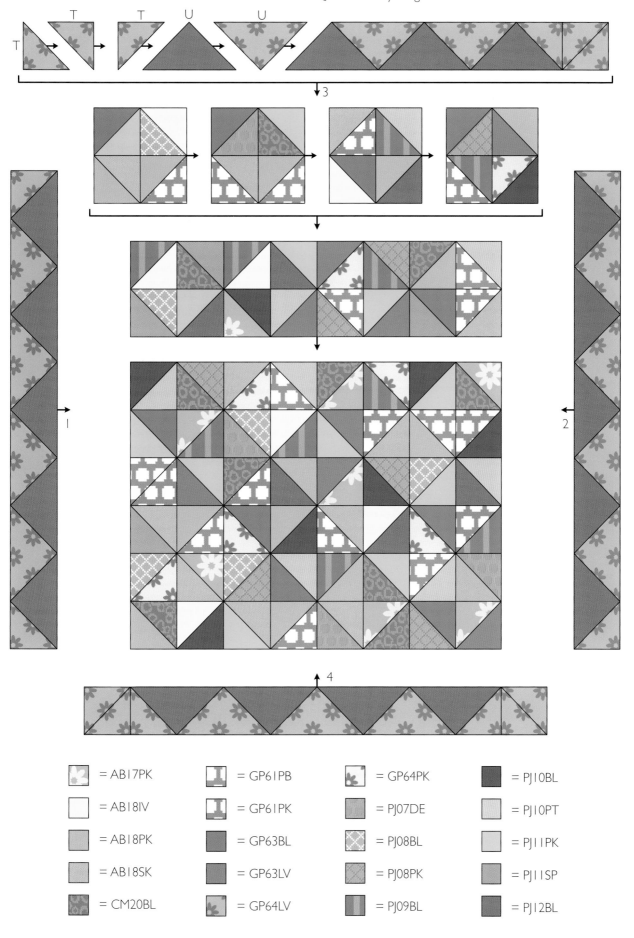

= AB17PK

= AB18IV

= AB18PK

= AB18SK

= CM20BL

= GP61PB

= GP61PK

= GP63BL

= GP63LV

= GP64LV

= GP64PK

= PJ07DE

= PJ08BL

= PJ08PK

= PJ09BL

= PJ10BL

= PJ10PT

= PJ11PK

= PJ11SP

= PJ12BL

Pastel Floral Parade Quilt ★

KAFFE FASSETT

Amy Butler's polka dot prints make joyous frames for this spring bouquet of a quilt. A perfect showcase for our new florals.

SIZE OF QUILT
The finished quilt will measure approx. 88in × 88in (223.5cm × 223.5cm).

MATERIALS
Patchwork Fabrics:

FULL MOON POLKA DOT
Camel	AB13CA:	¼yd (25cm)
Cherry	AB13CH:	⅜yd (35cm)
Lime	AB13LM:	⅜yd (35cm)
Slate	AB13SE:	⅜yd (35cm)
Tangerine	AB13TN:	⅜yd (35cm)

WATER LILY
Clay	AB15CY:	⅜yd (35cm)

TREE PEONY
Ivory	AB18IV:	⅝yd (60cm)

VERBENA
Pink	GP61PK:	⅝yd (60cm)

GERANIUM
Duck Egg	PJ07DE:	⅜yd (35cm)

MORNING GLORY
Gold	PJ08GD:	⅜yd (35cm)
Pink	PJ08PK:	⅜yd (35cm)

HOLLYHOCKS
Citron	PJ09CN:	⅜yd (35cm)

FOXGLOVES
Pastel	PJ10PT:	⅝yd (60cm)
Spring	PJ10SP:	⅜yd (35cm)

LUSCIOUS
Pink	PJ11PK:	1yd (90cm)
Spring	PJ11SP:	1yd (90cm)
Summer	PJ11SU:	¾yd (70cm)

SHOT COTTON
Rosy	SC32:	⅜yd (35cm)
Apple	SC39:	⅜yd (35cm)
Butter	SC64:	⅛yd (15cm)

Backing Fabric: 8¼yds (7.5m)
We suggest the following fabrics for backing:
PAISLEY JUNGLE Grey, GP60GY
VERBENA Pink, GP61PK
TREE PEONY Ivory, AB18IV

Binding:
FULL MOON POLKA DOT
Lime   AB13LM: ¾ yd (70cm)

Batting:
96in × 96in (244cm × 244cm).

Quilting thread:
Toning machine quilting thread

PATCH SHAPES
All the patches in this quilt are cut to size, no templates are provided as all the shapes are simple squares and rectangles. The centre panel is a large square, framed with sashing strips. This is surrounded by medium squares alternated with small squares framed with sashing strips.

CUTTING OUT
Cut the fabric in the order stated, starting with the largest patches. To reduce waste we suggest drawing out the patch shapes onto the reverse of the fabrics for the best fit before cutting.

Large Square: Cut 1 × 19½in (49.5cm) square in PJ11SP.

Medium Square: Cut 11½in (29.25cm) squares. Cut 6 in PJ11PK, 4 in PJ11SU, 3 in AB18IV, PJ10PT, PJ11SP, 2 in GP61PK, PJ07DE, PJ09CN, PJ10SP, 1 in AB15CY, PJ08GD and PJ08PK.

Small Square: Cut 8½in (21.5cm) squares. Cut 4 in GP61PK, PJ11PK, 3 in AB18IV, PJ10PT, PJ11SU, 2 in AB15CY, PJ07DE, PJ08GD, PJ09CN, PJ10SP, PJ11SP and 1 in PJ08PK.

For Sashing Strips D and C you can get 1 of each from a strip the width of the fabric.

Sashing Strip D: Cut 2in × 22½in (5cm × 57.25cm) strips. Cut 2 in AB13LM.

Sashing Strip C: Cut 2in × 19½in (5cm × 49.5cm) strips. Cut 2 in AB13LM.

For Sashing Strips B and A you can get 2 of each from a strip the width of the fabric.

Sashing Strip B: Cut 2in × 11½in (5cm × 29.25cm) strips. Cut 12 in SC39, 10 in SC32, 8 in AB13CH, AB13SE, AB13TN, 6 in AB13CA, 4 in AB13LM and SC64.

Sashing Strip A: Cut 2in × 8½in (5cm × 21.5cm) strips. Cut 12 in SC39, 10 in SC32, 8 in AB13CH, AB13SE, AB13TN, 6 in AB13CA, 4 in AB13LM and SC64.

Binding: Cut 9 strips 2½in (6.5cm) wide × width of fabric in AB13LM.

Backing: Cut 2 pieces 42in × 96in (106cm × 244cm) and 1 piece 13in × 96in (33cm × 244cm) in backing fabric.

MAKING THE BLOCKS
Use a ¼in (6mm) seam allowance throughout. Referring to the quilt assembly diagram for fabric placement piece 30 blocks as shown in the block assembly diagram using the small squares and sashing strips A and B. Also join sashing strips C and D to the large square in the same manner.

MAKING THE QUILT
Lay out the pieced blocks and alternately with the medium squares around the centre panel as shown in the quilt assembly diagram. Piece into rows and sections as shown, join the rows to complete the quilt.

FINISHING THE QUILT
Press the quilt top. Seam the backing pieces using a ¼in (6mm) seam allowance to form a piece approx. 96in × 96in (244cm × 244cm). Layer the quilt top, batting and backing and baste together (see page 139). Using toning machine quilting thread, quilt diagonally in both directions across each block, extending this lattice pattern across the centre block too. Trim the quilt edges and attach the binding (see page 140).

Block Assembly Diagram

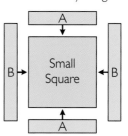

Quilt Assembly Diagram

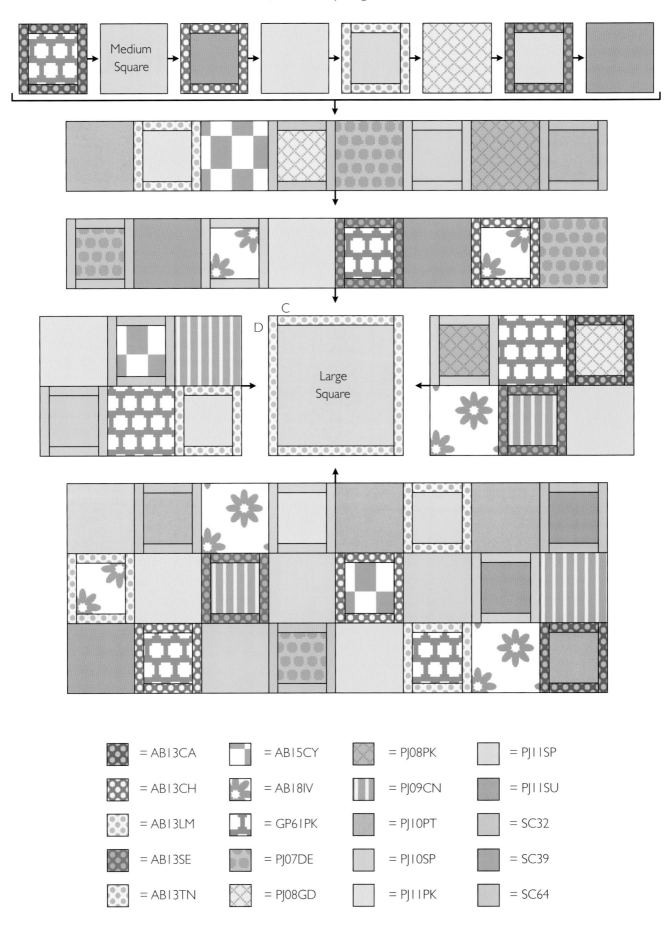

= AB13CA	= AB15CY	= PJ08PK	= PJ11SP
= AB13CH	= AB18IV	= PJ09CN	= PJ11SU
= AB13LM	= GP61PK	= PJ10PT	= SC32
= AB13SE	= PJ07DE	= PJ10SP	= SC39
= AB13TN	= PJ08GD	= PJ11PK	= SC64

Red Floral Parade Quilt ★

KAFFE FASSETT

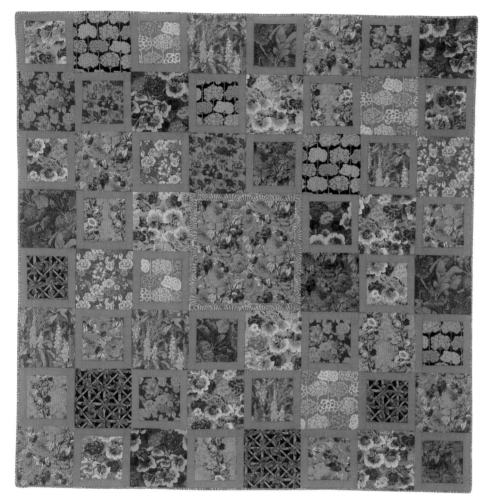

Taken from an old quilt layout, the sashing isolates and spotlights the prints in this jewel tone quilt very effectively.

SIZE OF QUILT
The finished quilt will measure approx. 88in × 88in (223.5cm × 223.5cm).

MATERIALS
Patchwork Fabrics:
PAPER FANS
Green   GP57GN: ⅛yd (15cm)
VERBENA
Brown   GP61BR: ⅜yd (35cm)
Red   GP61RD: ⅜yd (35cm)
MINTON
Maroon   GP63MR: ⅜yd (35cm)
Moss   GP63MS: ⅜yd (35cm)
Red   GP63RD: ⅜yd (35cm)

VEGETABLE LEAVES
Wine   MN05WN: ⅜yd (35cm)
GERANIUM
Lime   PJ07LM: ⅝yd (60cm)
Teal   PJ07TE: ⅝yd (60cm)
Tobacco   PJ07TO: ⅝yd (60cm)
MORNING GLORY
Purple   PJ08PU: ⅜yd (35cm)
HOLLYHOCKS
Sage   PJ09SA: ⅝yd (60cm)
FOXGLOVES
Red   PJ10RD: ⅝yd (60cm)
LUSCIOUS
Autumn   PJ11AT: ⅜yd (35cm)
Red   PJ11RD: 1¼yds (1.15m)

SHOT COTTON
Chartreuse   SC12: 1⅞yds (1.7m)

Backing Fabric: 8¼yds (7.5m)
We suggest the following fabrics for backing:
PAISLEY JUNGLE Rust, GP60RU
VERBENA Brown, GP61BR
HOLLYHOCKS Sage, PJ09SA

Binding:
PAPER FANS
Green   GP57GN: ¾ yd (70cm)

Batting:
96in × 96in (244cm × 244cm).

Quilting thread:
Toning machine quilting thread and dark red perlé cotton

PATCH SHAPES
See Pastel Floral Parade Quilt.

CUTTING OUT
Cut the fabric in the order stated, starting with the largest patches. To reduce waste we suggest drawing out the patch shapes onto the reverse of the fabrics for the best fit before cutting.
Large Square: Cut 1 × 19½in (49.5cm) square in PJ11RD.
Medium Square: Cut 11½in (29.25cm) squares. Cut 4 in PJ11RD, 3 in PJ07LM, PJ07TE, PJ07TO, PJ10RD, 2 in GP61BR, GP61RD, GP63MS, MN05WN, PJ08PU, 1 in GP63MR, GP63RD, PJ09SA and PJ11AT.
Small Square: Cut 8½in (21.5cm) squares. Cut 4 in PJ09SA, 3 in GP63MR, PJ07TO, PJ11RD, 2 in GP61BR, GP61RD, MN05WN, PJ07LM, PJ08PU, PJ10RD, PJ11AT, 1 in GP63MS, GP63RD and PJ07TE.
For Sashing Strips D and C you can get 1 of each from a strip the width of the fabric.
Sashing Strip D: Cut 2in × 22½in (5cm × 57.25cm) strips. Cut 2 in GP57GN.
Sashing Strip C: Cut 2in × 19½in (5cm × 49.5cm) strips. Cut 2 in GP57GN.
For Sashing Strips B and A you can get 2 of each from a strip the width of the fabric.
Sashing Strip B: Cut 2in × 11½in (5cm × 29.25cm) strips. Cut 60 in SC12.
Sashing Strip A: Cut 2in × 8½in (5cm × 21.5cm) strips. Cut 60 in SC12.

Binding: Cut 9 strips 2½in (6.5cm) wide × width of fabric in GP57GN.

Backing: Cut 2 pieces 42in × 96in (106cm × 244cm) and 1 piece 13in × 96in (33cm × 244cm) in backing fabric.

MAKING THE BLOCKS
See Pastel Floral Parade Quilt instructions.

MAKING THE QUILT
See Pastel Floral Parade Quilt instructions.

FINISHING THE QUILT
Press the quilt top. Seam the backing pieces using a ¼in (6mm) seam allowance to form a piece approx. 96in × 96in (244cm × 244cm). Layer the quilt top, batting and backing and baste together (see page 139). Using toning machine quilting thread, quilt in the ditch around the blocks. In the centre panel, free motion machine quilt following the flowers and foliage in the fabric. Using dark red perlé cotton hand quilt a square 3in (7.5cm) in from the block edge in the medium squares and 2in (5cm) in from the edge of the small squares. Trim the quilt edges and attach the binding (see page 140).

Quilt Assembly Diagram

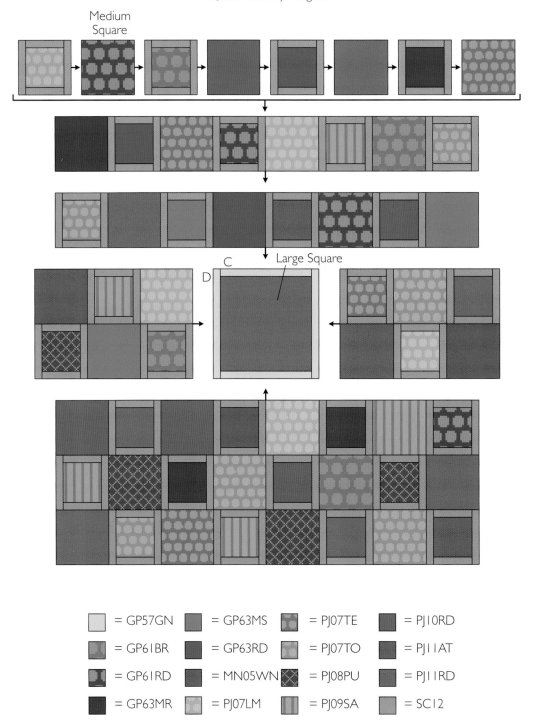

= GP57GN	= GP63MS	= PJ07TE	= PJ10RD
= GP61BR	= GP63RD	= PJ07TO	= PJ11AT
= GP61RD	= MN05WN	= PJ08PU	= PJ11RD
= GP63MR	= PJ07LM	= PJ09SA	= SC12

Delft Star Quilt ★★★

KAFFE FASSETT

I was thinking of the wonderful blue and white tile murals of Portugal as I designed this. As long as you keep it blue and white, any scrappy prints would work for this bold star – my blue Minton would be great, but it arrived just too late for this quilt.

SIZE OF QUILT
The finished quilt will measure approx. 60¼in x 60¼in (153cm x 153cm).

MATERIALS
Light Patchwork Fabrics, buy ¾ yd (70cm) of each
LAVA
Blue   CM01BL

DOT CUBE
Blue   CM04BL
CHICKEN SCRATCH
Shell   CM05SH
SHOT COTTON
Blush   SC28

Blue Patchwork Fabrics, buy ½ yd (45cm) of each.
BATIK CONFETTI

Blue   BKC02
STARSHINE
Blue   CM08BL
SWIRL MINI
Navy   CM10NV
BEAD STRIPE
Cobalt   GP50CB
WOVEN HAZE STRIPE
Aegean   HZS20

PLUMERIA
Blue   MN10BL
SHOT COTTON
Cobalt   SC45
Aegean   SC46

Setting and Border Fabrics:
FLOATING FLOWERS
Pastel   GP56PT: 1yd (90cm)
PAPER FANS
Cream   GP57CM: 1¾yds (1.6m)

Backing Fabric: 3⅞yds (3.5m)
We suggest the following fabrics for backing:
PAPER FANS Cream, GP57CM
FLOATING FLOWERS Pastel, GP56PT
MINTON Blue, GP63BL

Binding:
PLUMERIA
Blue   MN10BL: ½yd (45cm)

Batting:
68in x 68in (173cm x 173cm).

Quilting thread:
Toning machine quilting thread.

Template:

PP

PATCH SHAPES
The centre of this quilt is pieced using a diamond patch shape (Template PP). The diamonds are cut from fabrics which have been pieced into alternating blue and light strip sets. The diamonds are then pieced into 8 segments which are joined and the quilt centre is then completed using 4 setting squares and 4 setting triangles all cut to size. The quilt is completed with a simple border.

CUTTING OUT
Template PP: See Making the Diamonds section.
Setting Triangles: Cut 1 x 25in (63.5cm) square in GP57CM. Cut the square twice diagonally to form 4 triangles. This will ensure that the long side of the triangles do not have a bias edge. These setting triangles are cut oversize and will be trimmed after piecing.
Setting Squares: Cut 4 x 17in (43.25cm) squares in GP57CM. These setting squares are cut oversize and will be trimmed after piecing.
Borders: Cut 6 strips 5in (12.75cm) wide x width of fabric in GP56PT. Join the strips as necessary and cut 2 strips 63in x 5in (160cm x 12.75cm) for the side borders and 2 strips 53in x 5in (134.5cm x 12.75cm) for the top and bottom borders. These are a little oversized and will be trimmed to fit exactly later.
Binding: Cut 6 strips 2½in (6.5cm) wide x width of fabric in MN10BL.
Backing: Cut 1 piece 42in x 68in (106cm x 172.75cm) and 1 piece 25in x 68in (63.5cm x 172.75cm) in backing fabric.

MAKING THE DIAMONDS
There are 2 types of pieced diamonds (template PP) in this quilt, 'standard'

Cutting Diagrams

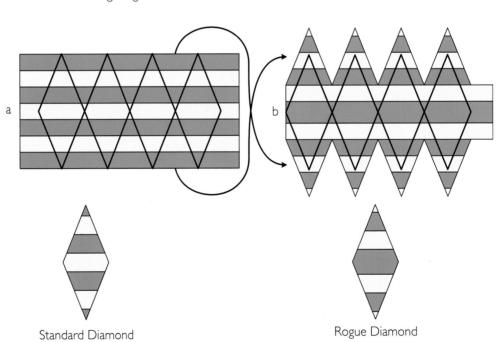

a   b

Standard Diamond   Rogue Diamond

Segment Assembly Diagram

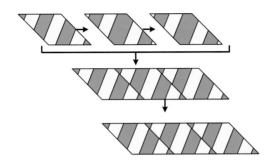

Quilt Centre Assembly Diagram

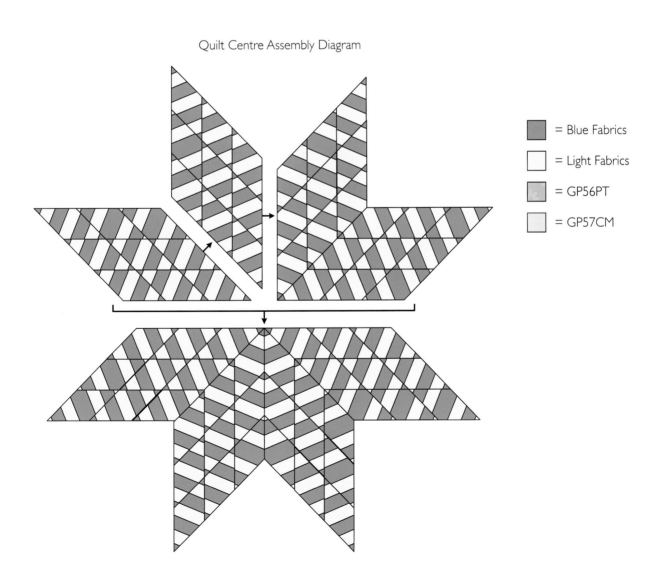

= Blue Fabrics

= Light Fabrics

= GP56PT

= GP57CM

diamonds, which have 3 light and 4 blue alternating fabrics, and 'rogue' diamonds which are much more varied in composition, using alternating light and blue fabrics, but varying widths of strip. These are pieced from wider strips and leftover cuttings from the 'standard' diamonds. The 'standard' diamonds are used in the centre of the star and the 'rogue' diamonds are introduced at the edges of the star. Look carefully at the photograph and choose fabrics in similar combinations for the strip sets. The centre ring of diamonds is important visually, so look carefully at the positions of the fabrics before piecing.

We suggest cutting and piecing as you go for this quilt. Cut all the light and blue fabrics in half down the length of the fabric so that you have 2 sections approx. 21in (53.5cm) wide. This allows for more variety in combinations of fabrics for the strip sets and easier handling of strips.

For the 'standard' diamonds cut 2in (5cm) strips across the width of the fabrics. Piece the strips alternating the light and blue fabrics as shown in cutting diagram a. Note: Fabric CM04BL was used mostly with the wrong side up. Cut 4 diamonds from each strip set using template PP as shown. Make up enough strip sets for 54 'standard' diamonds.

For the 'rogue' diamonds cut some extra strips across the width of the fabric, these can vary from 2½in to 3in (6.35cm to 7.75cm). Combine these strips with the leftover cuttings from the 'standard' diamonds as shown in cutting diagram b. This diagram is meant as a guide, you can vary your strips much more if you wish. Cut a total of 18 'rogue' diamonds.

MAKING THE QUILT
Using a design wall to arrange your diamonds lay out the whole quilt centre. Separate the diamonds into 8 segments and piece as

shown in the segment assembly diagram. Join the segments as shown in the quilt centre assembly diagram. Add the setting triangles and setting squares using the inset seams method (see Patchwork Know How on page 138). Trim the edges to ¼in (6mm) OUTSIDE the star points. Finally trim the top and bottom borders to fit and join to the quilt centre, then trim the side borders and join to the quilt centre.

FINISHING THE QUILT
Press the quilt top. Seam the backing pieces using a ¼in (6mm) seam allowance to form a piece approx. 68in x 68in (173cm x 173cm). Layer the quilt top, batting and backing and baste together (see page 139). Using toning machine quilting thread, quilt in the ditch around the diamonds. In the setting squares and triangles free motion quilt following the curves of the fan shapes and in the border free motion quilt around the flowers. Trim the quilt edges and attach the binding (see page 140).

Quilt Assembly Diagram

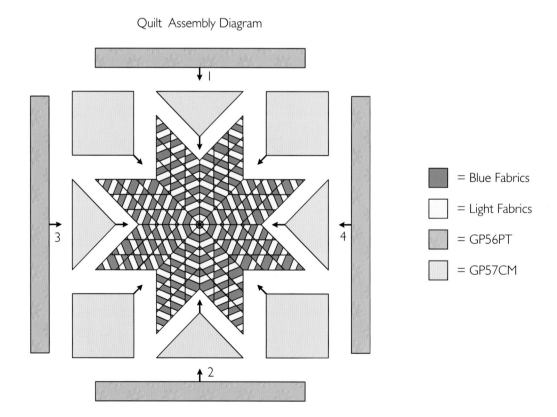

= Blue Fabrics

= Light Fabrics

= GP56PT

= GP57CM

Perkiomen Valley Quilt ★★★

LIZA PRIOR LUCY

In the next county over from where I live is an area called the Perkiomen Valley. It isn't far from Amish country and quilting there is a long practised art. This quilt is a variation of the locally popular 'split 9—patch' traditional quilt called Perkiomen Valley.

SIZE OF QUILT
The finished quilt will measure approx. 75in x 90in (190.5cm x 228.5cm).

MATERIALS
This fabric list is a guide, don't worry about substituting other fabrics in if some are not available. Some of these fabrics are large prints and different areas of the design have light and dark parts, you can therefore use some in both light and dark positions. Sort the fabric patches by tone and colour after cutting.
Buy ¼yd (25cm) of each of the following fabrics.

Light patchwork Fabrics:
FISH Lavender	CM11LV
URCHINS Lavender	CM12LV
SHELLS Sand	CM13SN
BASKET STRIPE Lavender	CM14LV
CORAL FLOWERS Sand	CM15SN
PAPERWEIGHT Sludge	GP20SL
PAPERWEIGHT Pastel	GP20PT
ORGANIC DOTS Mint	GP53MT
DAHLIA BLOOM Succulent	GP54SC
FLOATING FLOWERS Pastel	GP56PT
FLOATING FLOWERS Mauve	GP56MV

SAMARKAND Stone	GP58ST
SAMARKAND Frost	GP58FR
GUINEA FLOWER Mauve	GP59MV
PAISLEY JUNGLE Grey	GP60GY
RIBBONS & BOWS Purple	MN14PU

Dark Patchwork Fabrics:

FISH Royal	CM11RY
FISH Teal	CM11TE
URCHINS Purple	CM12PU
URCHINS Royal	CM12RY
URCHINS Teal	CM12TE
SHELLS Black	CM13BK
BASKET STRIPE Teal	CM14TE
CORAL FLOWERS Green	CM15GN
PAPERWEIGHT Algae	GP20AL
EMBROIDERED LEAF Taupe	
	GP42TA
CLOISONNE Moss	GP46MS
CLOISONNE Teal	GP46TE
SHIRT STRIPES Soft	GP51SF
AURICULA Green	GP52GN
AURICULA Olive	GP52OV
FLOATING FLOWERS Green	
	GP56GN
GUINEA FLOWER Green	GP59GN

SHOT COTTON

Apple	SC39: 1yd (90cm)

Backing Fabric: 5¾yds (5.25m)
We suggest these fabrics for backing:
SAMARKAND Stone, GP58ST
PAPERWEIGHT Algae, GP20AL
BASKET STRIPE Lavender, CM14LV

Binding:
BASKET STRIPE
Royal   CM14RY: ⅞yd (80cm)

Batting:
83in × 98in (211cm × 249cm).

Quilting thread:
Sage green machine quilting thread.

Templates:

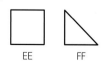

EE   FF

PATCH SHAPES
This split 9–patch block which finishes to 7½in (19cm) is made using 1 square patch shape (Template EE) and 1 triangle patch shape (Template FF). The blocks are straight set into rows. Using a design wall to lay out

the fabrics for this quilt will help to get the soft colourwash effect that Liza achieved. We have included information about design walls in the glossary at the back of the book.

CUTTING OUT
Template EE: Cut 3in (7.6cm) strips across the width of the fabric. Each strip will give you 14 patches per 45in (114cm) wide fabric. Cut a total of 360 in light fabric, 360 in dark fabric and 120 in SC39.
Template FF: Cut 3⅜in (8.5cm) strips across the width of the fabric. Each strip will give you 24 patches per 45in (114cm) wide fabric. Cut a total of 240 in light fabric and, 240 in dark fabric.

Binding: Cut 9⅝yds (8.8m) of 2½in (6.5cm) wide bias binding in CM14RY.

Backing: Cut 2 pieces 42in × 98in (106.5cm × 249cm) backing fabric.

MAKING THE BLOCKS
Use a ¼in (6mm) seam allowance throughout. For each block take 3 light, 3

dark and 1 SC39 template EE square, 2 light and 2 dark template FF triangle. Each fabric should be different. Following block assembly diagram a, piece the triangles into 2 squares. Then arrange the pieced squares with the other patches as shown in diagram b and piece. The finished block can be seen in diagram c. Piece a total of 120 blocks.

MAKING THE QUILT
Lay out all the blocks as shown in the quilt assembly diagram. Check that the overall pattern is correct by standing back. Join the blocks into 12 rows of 10 blocks. Join the rows to form the quilt.

FINISHING THE QUILT
Press the quilt top. Seam the backing pieces using a ¼in (6mm) seam allowance to form a piece approx. 83in × 98in (211cm × 249cm). Layer the quilt top, batting and backing and baste together (see page 139). Using sage green machine quilting thread, meander quilt with swirling random shapes across the surface of the quilt. Trim the quilt edges and attach the binding (see page 140).

Block Assembly Diagrams

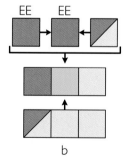

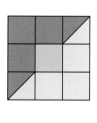

a   b   c

Quilt Assembly Diagram

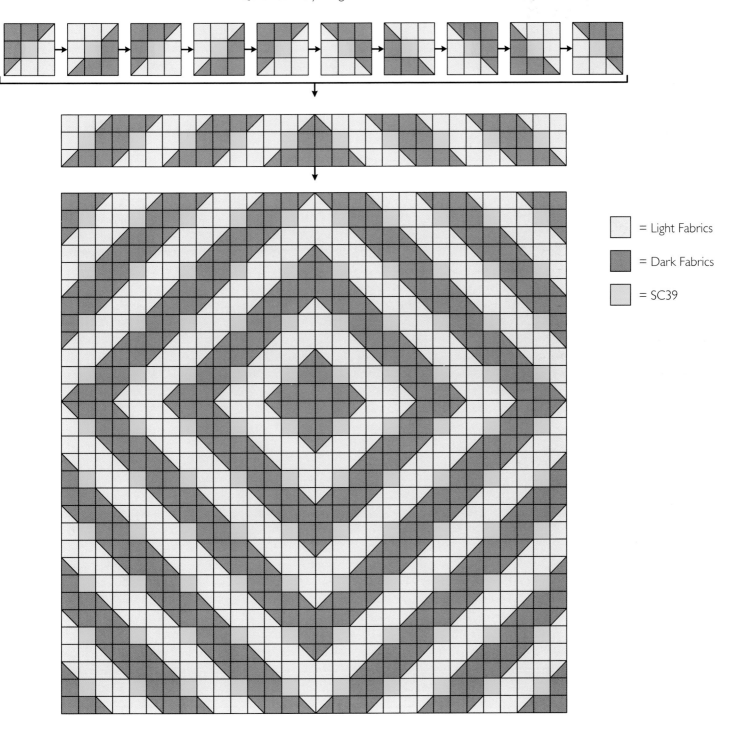

= Light Fabrics

= Dark Fabrics

= SC39

Blue Portugal Quilt ★★

LIZA PRIOR LUCY

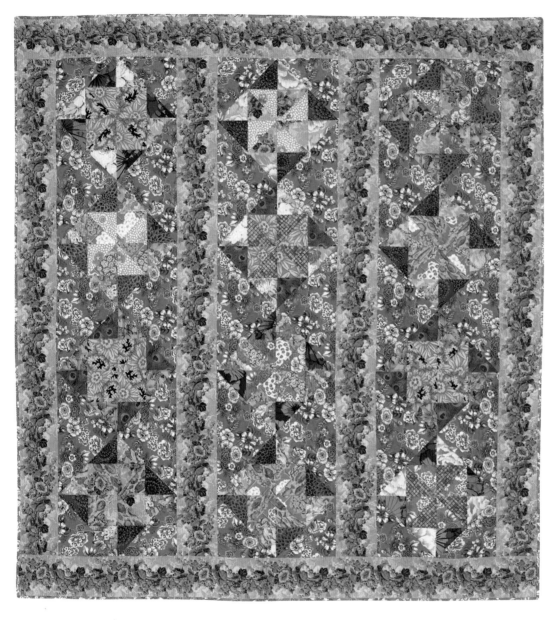

Blue and white is a much loved, easy to live with colour combination. The tiles of Portugal provide a great backdrop for this blue and white classic strippy quilt.

SIZE OF QUILT

The finished quilt will measure approx. 74in x 79½in (188cm x 202cm).

MATERIALS

Patchwork, Sashing and Border Fabrics:

FISH		
Lavender	CM11LV:	¼yd (25cm)
TILES		
Teal	CM19TE:	¼yd (25cm)
PEACOCK FEATHERS		
Blue	CM22BL:	¼yd (25cm)

LOTUS LEAF		
Blue	GP29BL:	¼yd (25cm)
KIMONO		
Pink/Orange	GP33PO:	¼yd (25cm)
DAHLIA BLOOMS		
Cool	GP54CL:	¼yd (25cm)
FLOATING FLOWERS		
Blue	GP56BL:	¼yd (25cm)
GUINEA FLOWER		
Mauve	GP59MV:	¼yd (25cm)
VERBENA		
Powder Blue	GP61PB:	¼yd (25cm)

MINTON		
Blue	GP63BL:	2¼yds (2.1m)
Lavender	GP63LV:	¼yd (25cm)
POTENTILLA		
Blue	GP64BL:	¼yd (25cm)
MORNING GLORY		
Cerulean	PJ08CE:	¼yd (25cm)
HOLLYHOCKS		
Blue	PJ09BL:	2¼yds (2.1m)
FOXGLOVE		
Pastel	PJ10PT:	¼yd (25cm)
LUSCIOUS		

Pink   PJ11PK: ¼yd (25cm)
CORAL LEAF
Blue   PJ12BL: ¼yd (25cm)

Backing Fabric: 4¾yds (4.35m)
We suggest these fabrics for backing:
FLORAL STRIPE Royal, GP62RY
POTENTILLA Blue, GP64BL
MORNING GLORY Cerulean, PJ08CE

Binding:
MINTON
Lavender   GP63LV: ¾ yd (70cm)

Batting:
82in × 88in (208cm × 223.5cm).

Quilting thread:
Pale blue machine quilting thread.

Templates:

Z   Corner Setting   Side Setting
      Triangle   Triangle

PATCH SHAPES
Pinwheel Blocks made using 1 triangle patch shape (Template Z) are set 'on point' into columns using 2 triangle patch shapes (Side Setting Triangle and Corner Setting Triangle) which are cut to size. The pieced columns are interspaced with 2 sashing strips and then surrounded with a simple border.

CUTTING OUT
Sashing and Borders: These are fussy cut down the length of the fabric to centre the floral hollyhocks design, see the photograph for more details. Cut 2 strips 6¼in × 68½in (15.9cm × 174cm) in PJ09BL. These strips must be cut along each of the selvedge edges of the fabric and will be the side borders.
Cut 2 strips 6¼in × 68½in (15.9cm × 174cm) in PJ09BL for the inner sashing strips.
Cut 2 strips 6¼in × 74½in (15.9cm × 189.25cm) in PJ09BL for the top and bottom borders. Reserve leftover fabric for template Z.
Side Setting Triangles: Make a paper template by cutting a 12⅞in (32.75cm) square, then folding diagonally to form a right–angle triangle. The straight grain of the fabric must run along the long side of the triangle, this will ensure the long side of the triangle will not have a bias edge. Cut 6 strips 9⅛in (23.25cm) wide across the width of the

fabric. Each strip will give you 3 patches per 45in (114cm) wide fabric. Cut 18 in GP63BL.
Corner Setting Triangles: Cut 9⅜in (23.75cm) wide strips across the width of the fabric. Each strip will give you 8 patches per 45in (114cm) wide fabric. Cut 9⅜in (23.75cm) squares, cut each square diagonally to form 2 triangles, cut 12 in GP63BL.
Template Z: Fabric PJ09BL only, using the leftover fabric from the sashing and borders cut 12 ensuring the grain of the fabric is along the long side of the triangles.
Other fabrics: Cut 7¼in (18.5cm) wide strips across the width of the fabric. Each strip will give you 20 patches per 45in (114cm) wide fabric. Cut 7¼in (18.5cm) squares, then cut each square twice diagonally to make 4 triangles, using the template as a guide. This will ensure the long side of the triangle will not have a bias edge. Note: do not move the patches until both diagonals have been cut. Cut 16 in GP61PB, GP64BL, PJ10PT, 12 in CM11LV, CM22BL, GP29BL, GP54CL, GP56BL, GP63LV, PJ08CE, PJ11PK, PJ12BL, 8 in CM19TE, GP33PO and GP59MV.

Binding: Cut 8 strips 2½in (6.5cm) wide across the width of the fabric in GP63LV.

Backing: Cut 2 pieces 44in × 82in (112cm × 208cm) in backing fabric.

MAKING THE BLOCKS AND PIECED COLUMNS
Use a ¼in (6mm) seam allowance throughout. Piece 12 blocks following block assembly diagram a and b, the finished block can be seen in diagram c. Refer to the quilt assembly diagram for fabric placement. Piece the blocks together into 3 rows of 4 blocks using the Side and Corner Setting Triangles to set the blocks 'on point' as shown in the quilt assembly diagram.

MAKING THE QUILT
Lay out the pieced columns interspaced with the inner sashing strips and join as shown in the quilt assembly diagram. Add the side, then top and bottom borders to complete the quilt.

FINISHING THE QUILT
Press the quilt top. Seam the backing pieces using a ¼in (6mm) seam allowance to form a piece approx. 82in × 88in (208cm × 223.5cm). Layer the quilt top, batting and backing and baste together (see page 139). Using pale blue machine quilting thread, quilt in the ditch in the block seams, around the blocks and in the sashing seams, then free style quilt following the flowers and foliage in the sashing strips and borders. Trim the quilt edges and attach the binding (see page 140).

Block Assembly Diagrams

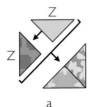

a

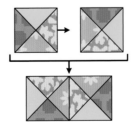

b

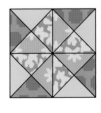

c

Quilt Assembly Diagram

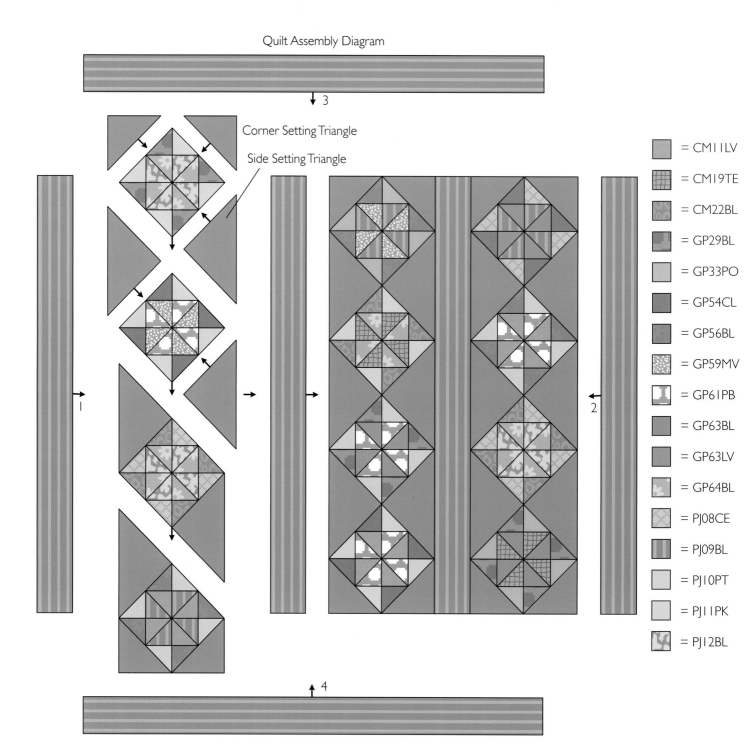

Corner Setting Triangle

Side Setting Triangle

3

1

2

4

= CM11LV

= CM19TE

= CM22BL

= GP29BL

= GP33PO

= GP54CL

= GP56BL

= GP59MV

= GP61PB

= GP63BL

= GP63LV

= GP64BL

= PJ08CE

= PJ09BL

= PJ10PT

= PJ11PK

= PJ12BL

TEMPLATES

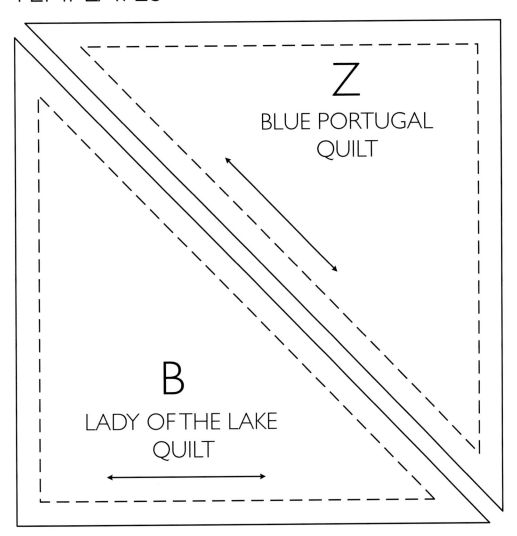

Z
BLUE PORTUGAL
QUILT

B
LADY OF THE LAKE
QUILT

E
OCTAGONS WITH
STARS QUILT

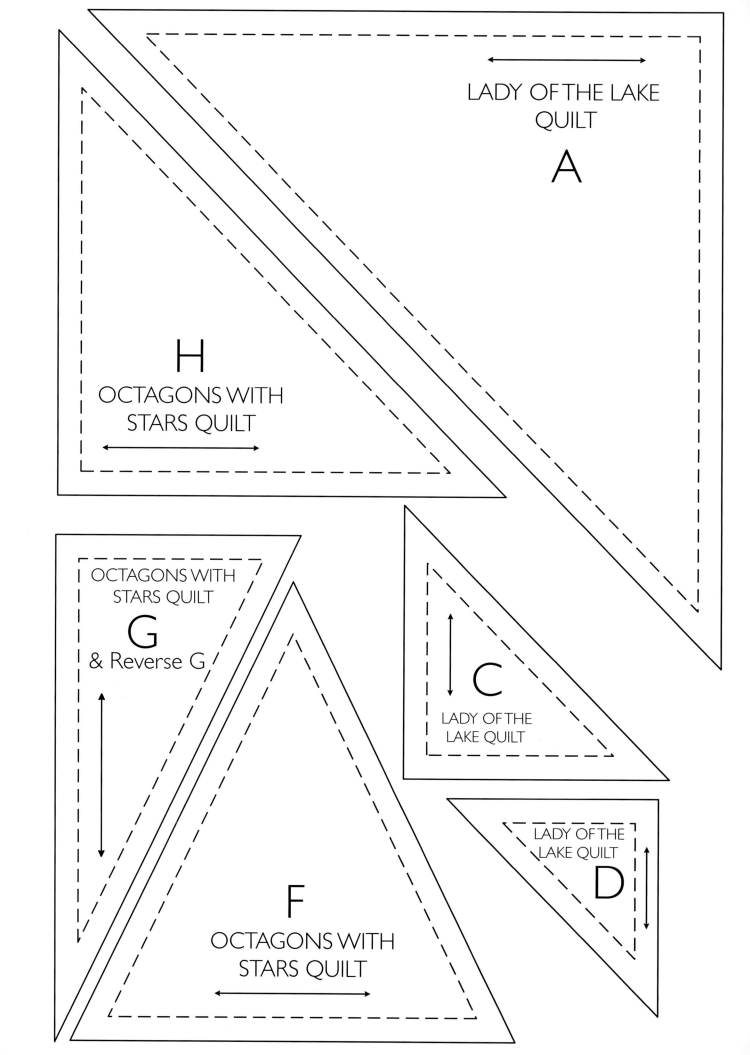

LADY OF THE LAKE
QUILT

A

H
OCTAGONS WITH
STARS QUILT

OCTAGONS WITH
STARS QUILT

G

& Reverse G

C

LADY OF THE
LAKE QUILT

LADY OF THE
LAKE QUILT

D

F
OCTAGONS WITH
STARS QUILT

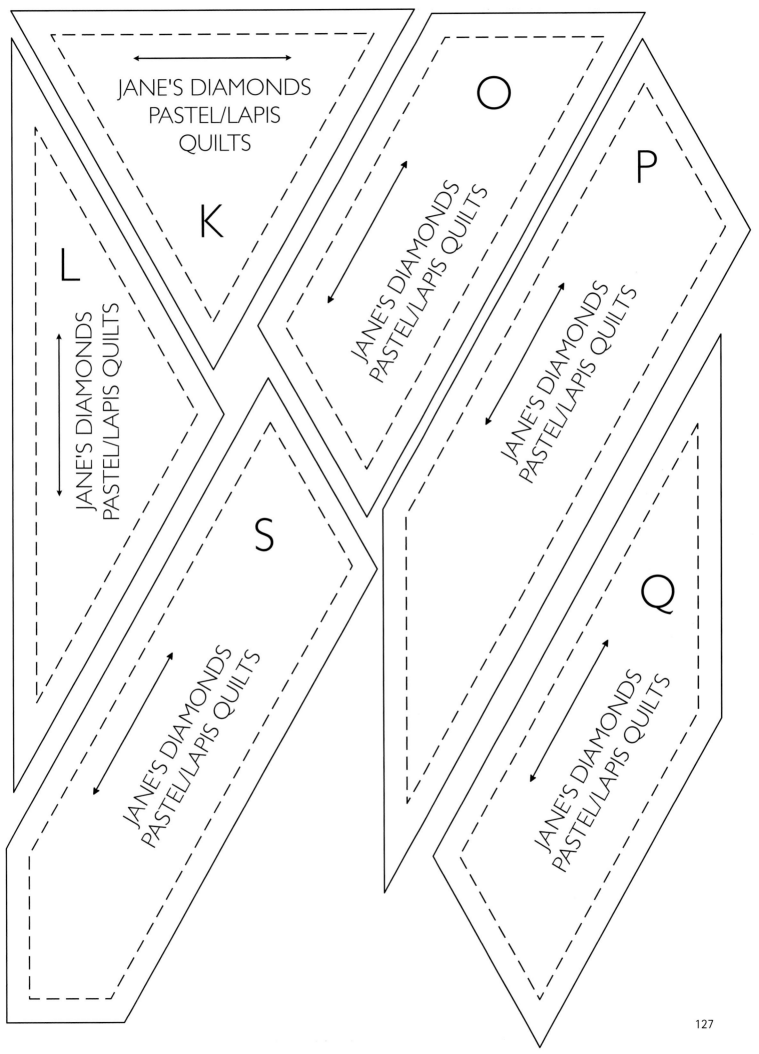

JANE'S DIAMONDS
PASTEL/LAPIS
QUILTS

K

O

P

L

JANE'S DIAMONDS PASTEL/LAPIS QUILTS

JANE'S DIAMONDS PASTEL/LAPIS QUILTS

JANE'S DIAMONDS PASTEL/LAPIS QUILTS

S

JANE'S DIAMONDS PASTEL/LAPIS QUILTS

Q

JANE'S DIAMONDS PASTEL/LAPIS QUILTS

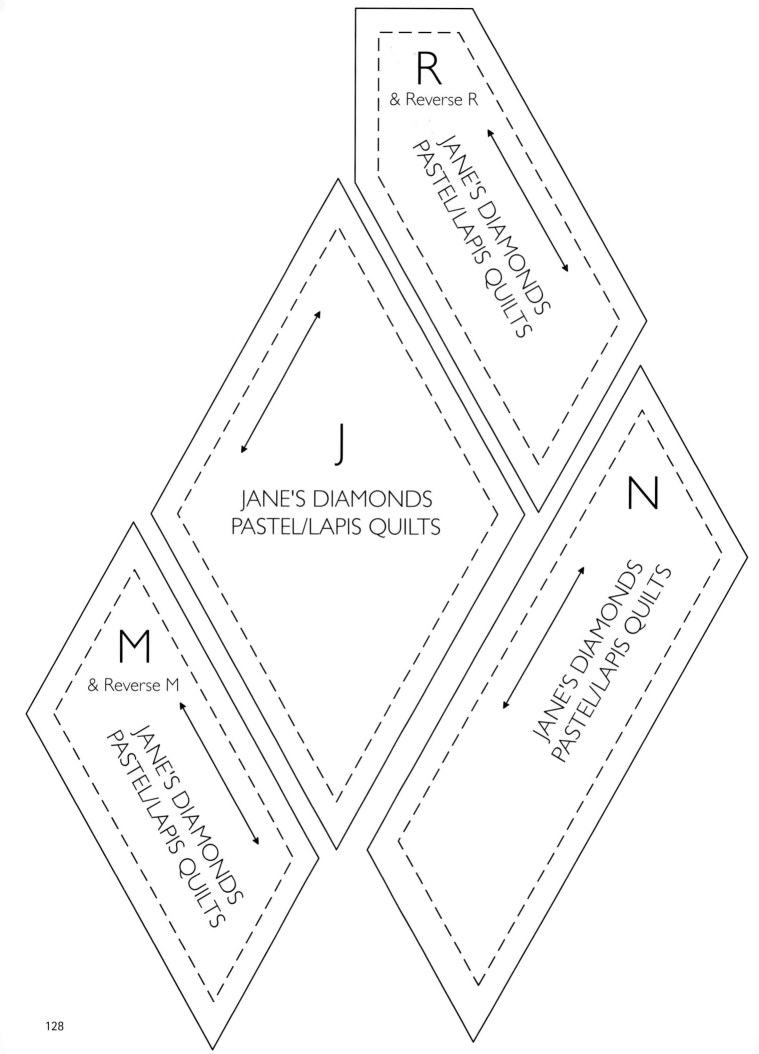

R
& Reverse R

JANE'S DIAMONDS
PASTEL/LAPIS QUILTS

J

JANE'S DIAMONDS
PASTEL/LAPIS QUILTS

N

JANE'S DIAMONDS
PASTEL/LAPIS QUILTS

M
& Reverse M

JANE'S DIAMONDS
PASTEL/LAPIS QUILTS

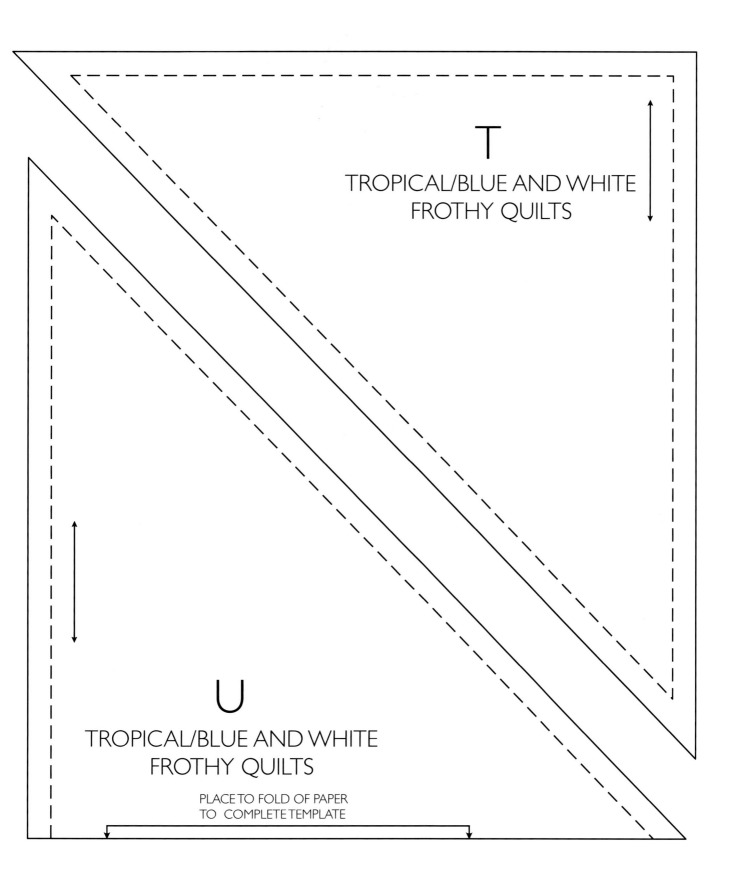

T

TROPICAL/BLUE AND WHITE
FROTHY QUILTS

U

TROPICAL/BLUE AND WHITE
FROTHY QUILTS

PLACE TO FOLD OF PAPER
TO COMPLETE TEMPLATE

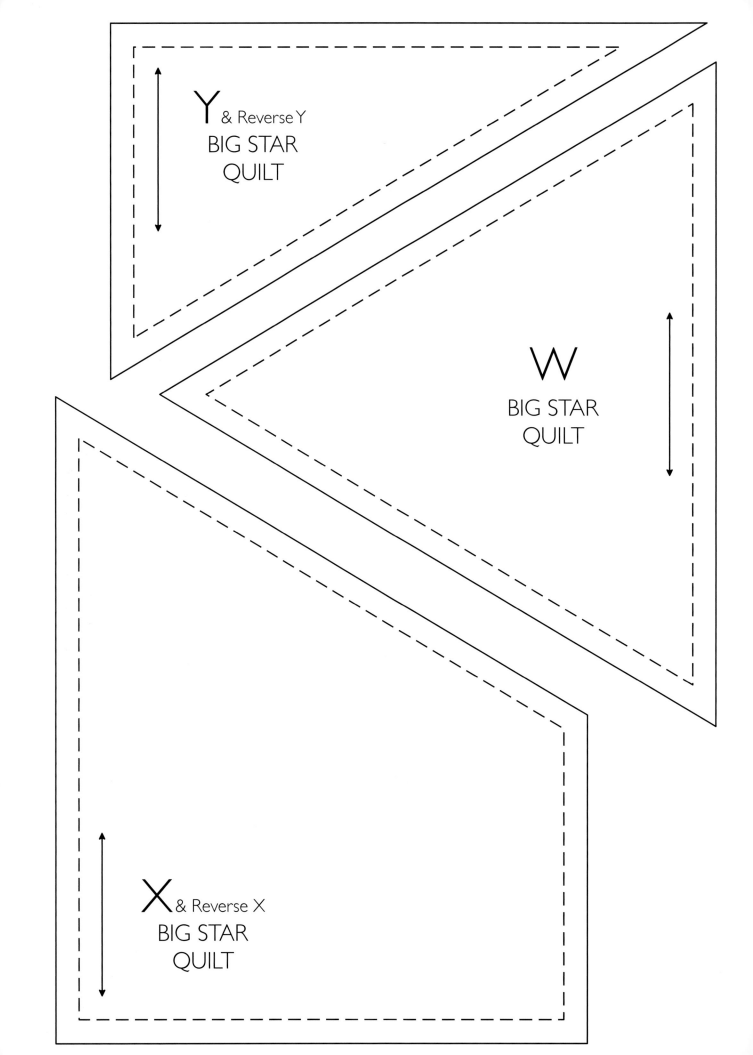

Y & Reverse Y
BIG STAR
QUILT

W
BIG STAR
QUILT

X & Reverse X
BIG STAR
QUILT

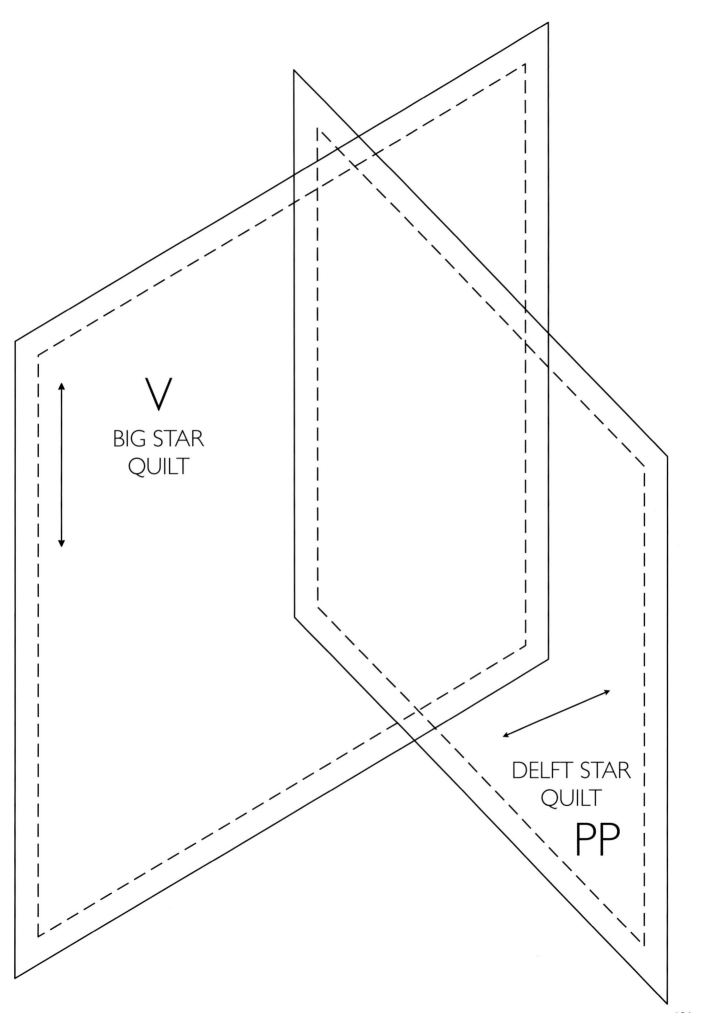

V
BIG STAR
QUILT

DELFT STAR
QUILT

PP

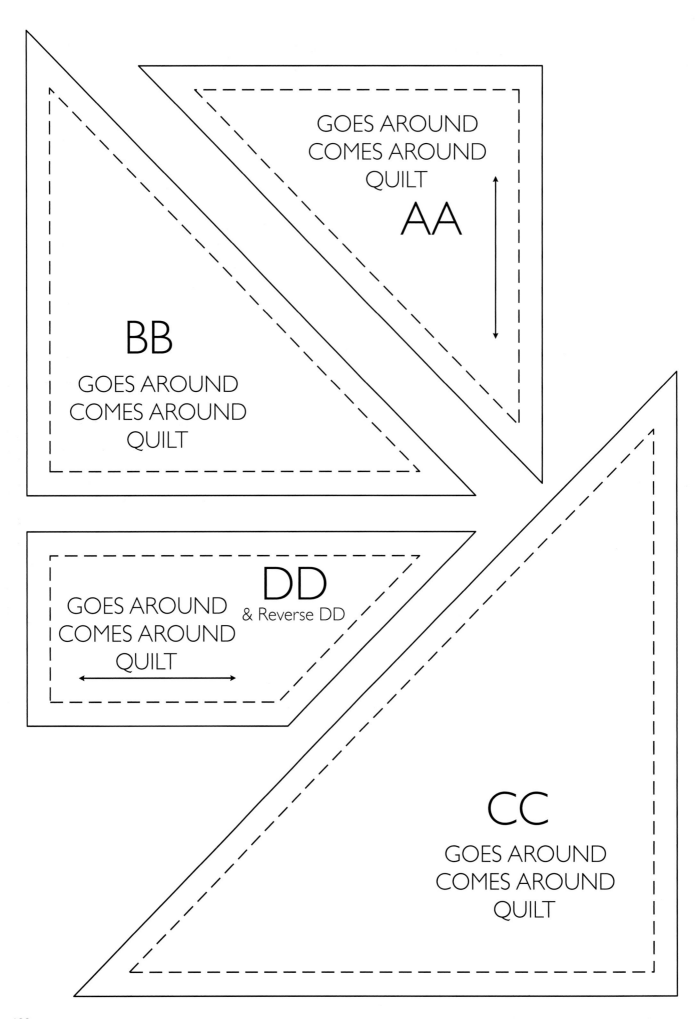

GOES AROUND
COMES AROUND
QUILT
AA

BB
GOES AROUND
COMES AROUND
QUILT

DD
& Reverse DD

GOES AROUND
COMES AROUND
QUILT

CC
GOES AROUND
COMES AROUND
QUILT

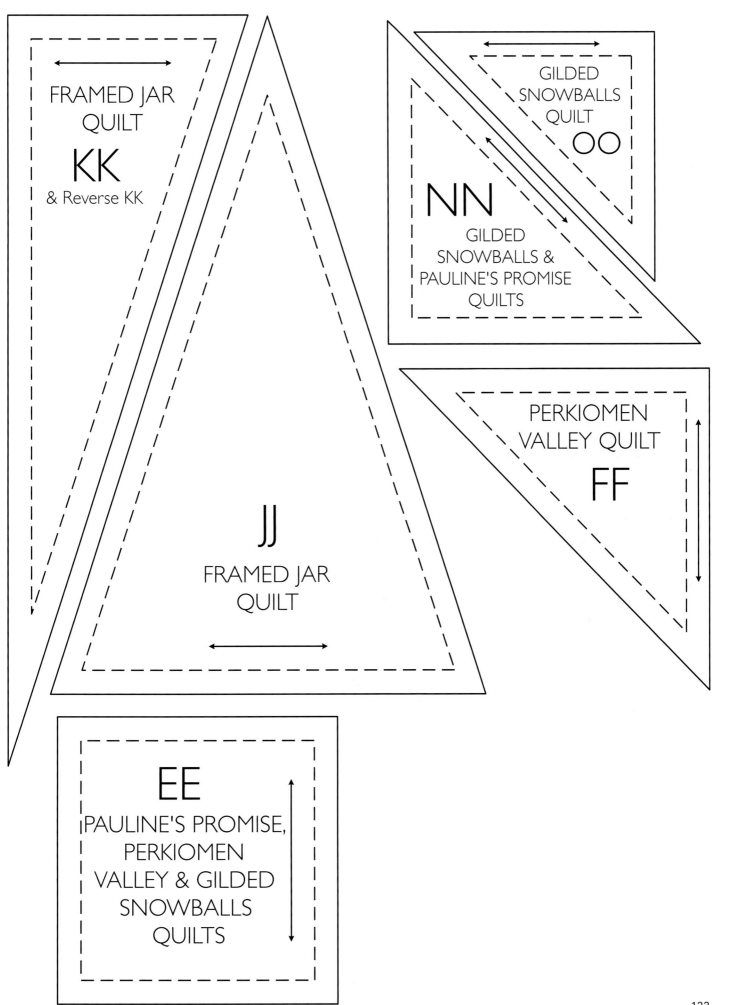

FRAMED JAR
QUILT

KK

& Reverse KK

GILDED
SNOWBALLS
QUILT

OO

NN

GILDED
SNOWBALLS &
PAULINE'S PROMISE
QUILTS

PERKIOMEN
VALLEY QUILT

FF

JJ

FRAMED JAR
QUILT

EE

PAULINE'S PROMISE,
PERKIOMEN
VALLEY & GILDED
SNOWBALLS
QUILTS

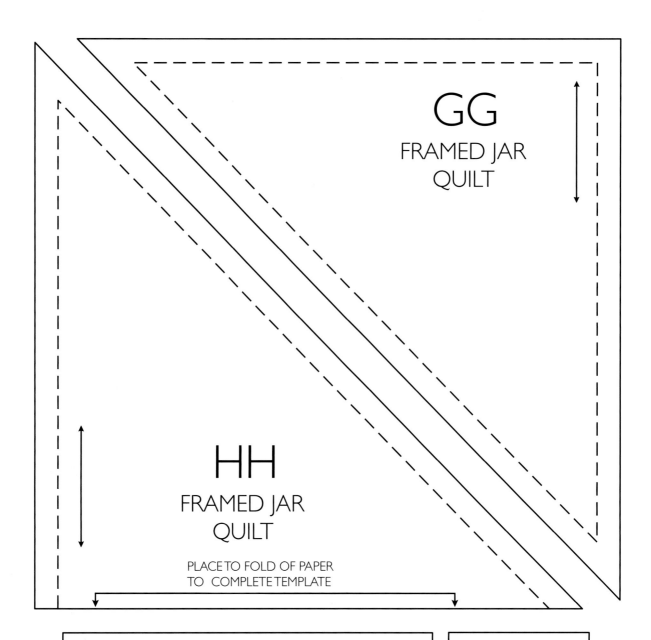

GG
FRAMED JAR
QUILT

HH
FRAMED JAR
QUILT

PLACE TO FOLD OF PAPER
TO COMPLETE TEMPLATE

GILDED
SNOWBALLS
QUILT
LL

GILDED
SNOWBALLS
QUILT
MM

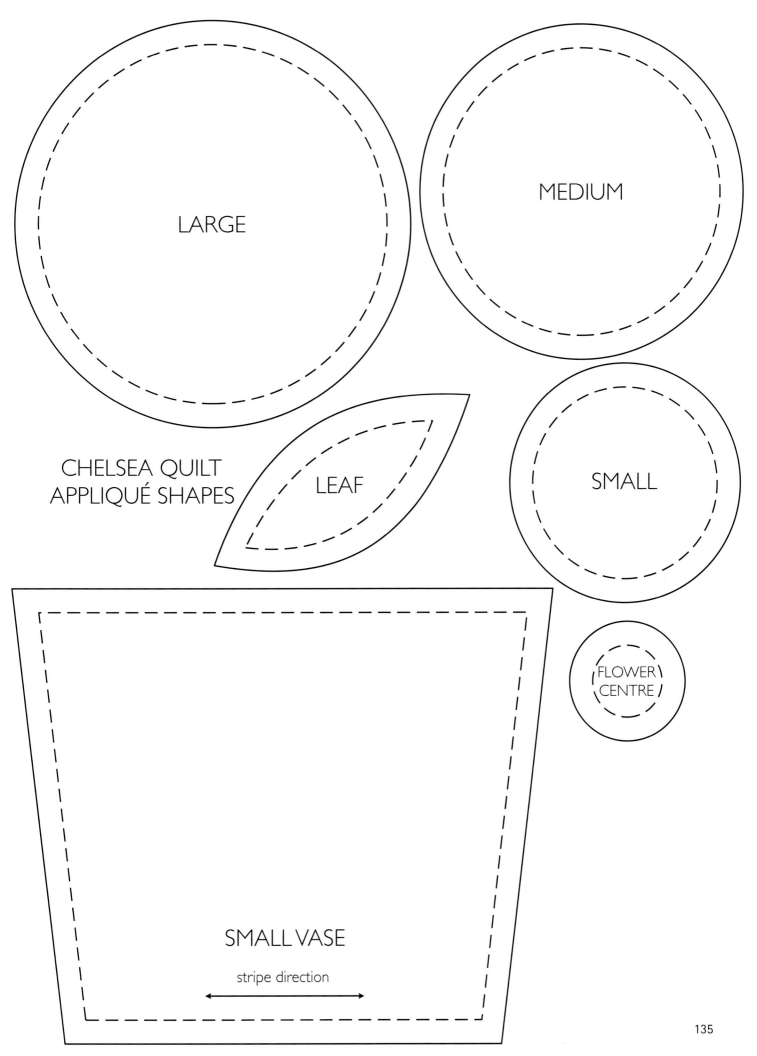

LARGE

MEDIUM

CHELSEA QUILT
APPLIQUÉ SHAPES

LEAF

SMALL

FLOWER
CENTRE

SMALL VASE

stripe direction

135

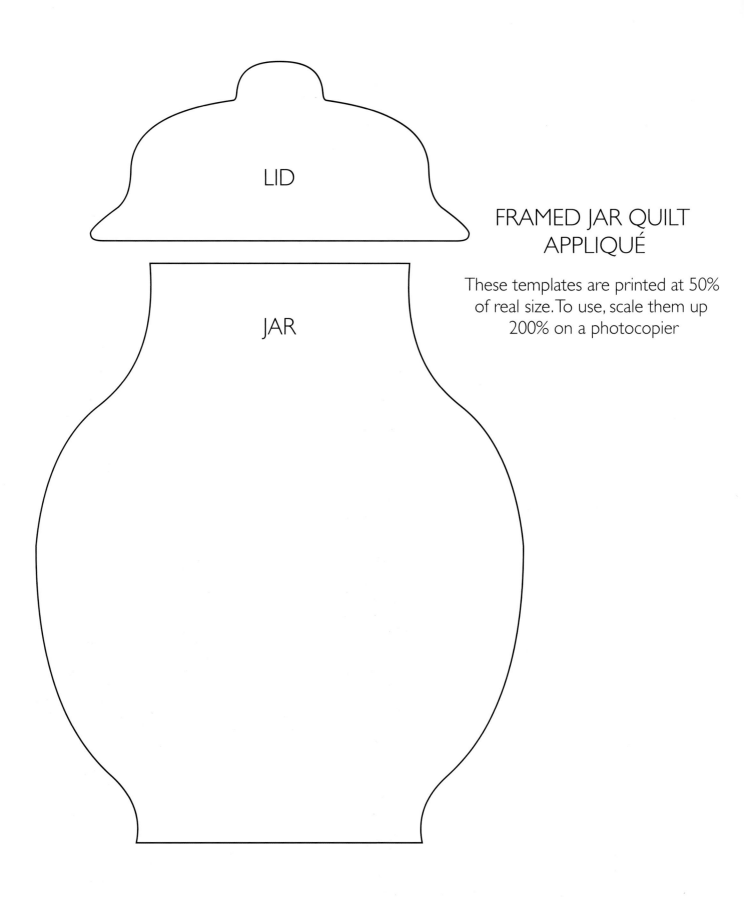

LID

JAR

FRAMED JAR QUILT
APPLIQUÉ

These templates are printed at 50% of real size. To use, scale them up 200% on a photocopier

Patchwork Know How

These instructions are intended for the novice quilt maker, providing the basic information needed to make the projects in this book, along with some useful tips.

Preparing the fabric

Prewash all new fabrics before you begin, to ensure that there will be no uneven shrinkage and no bleeding of colours when the quilt is laundered. Press the fabric whilst it is still damp to return crispness to it.

Making templates

Transparent template plastic is the best material, it is durable and allows you to see the fabric and select certain motifs. You can also use thin stiff cardboard.

Templates for machine piecing

1 Trace off the actual-sized template provided either directly on to template plastic, or tracing paper, and then on to thin cardboard. Use a ruler to help you trace off the straight cutting line, dotted seam line and grainlines. Some of the templates in this book are so large that we have only been able to give you half of them. Before transferring them on to plastic or card, trace off the half template, place the fold edge up to the fold of a piece of paper, and carefully draw around the shape. Cut out the paper double thickness, and open out for the completed template.

2 Cut out the traced off template using a craft knife, ruler and a self-healing cutting mat.

3 Punch holes in the corners of the template, at each point on the seam line, using a hole punch.

Templates for hand piecing

• Make a template as for machine piecing, but do not trace off the cutting line. Use the dotted seam line as the outer edge of the template.

• This template allows you to draw the seam lines directly on to the fabric. The seam allowances can then be cut by eye around the patch.

Cutting the fabric

On the individual instructions for each patchwork, you will find a summary of all the patch shapes used.
Always mark and cut out any border and binding strips first, followed by the largest patch shapes and finally the smallest ones, to make the most efficient use of your fabric. The border and binding strips are best cut using a rotary cutter.

Rotary cutting

Rotary cut strips are usually cut across the fabric from selvedge to selvedge, but some projects may vary, so please read through all the instructions before you start cutting the fabrics.

1 Before beginning to cut, press out any folds or creases in the fabric. If you are cutting a large piece of fabric, you will need to fold it several times to fit the cutting mat. When there is only a single fold, place the fold facing you. If the fabric is too wide to be folded only once, fold it concertina-style until it fits your mat. A small rotary cutter with a sharp blade will cut up to 6 layers of fabric; a large cutter up to 8 layers.

2 To ensure that your cut strips are straight and even, the folds must be placed exactly parallel to the straight edges of the fabric and along a line on the cutting mat.

3 Place a plastic ruler over the raw edge of the fabric, overlapping it about ½in (1.25cm). Make sure that the ruler is at right angles to both the straight edges and the fold to ensure that you cut along the straight grain. Press down on the ruler and wheel the cutter away from yourself along the edge of the ruler.

4 Open out the fabric to check the edge. Don't worry if it's not perfectly straight; a little wiggle will not show when the quilt is stitched together. Re-fold fabric, then place the ruler over the trimmed edge, aligning edge with the markings on the ruler that match the correct strip width. Cut strip along the edge of the ruler.

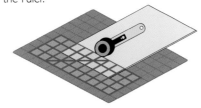

Using templates

The most efficient way to cut out templates is by first rotary cutting a strip of fabric the width stated for your template, and then marking off your templates along the strip, edge to edge at the required angle. This method leaves hardly any waste and gives a random effect to your patches.
A less efficient method is to fussy cut, where the templates are cut individually by placing them on particular motifs or stripes, to create special effects. Although this method is more wasteful it yields very interesting results.

1 Place the template face down on the wrong side of the fabric, with the grain line arrow following the straight grain of the fabric, if indicated. Be careful though - check with your individual instructions, as some instructions may ask you to cut patches on varying grains.

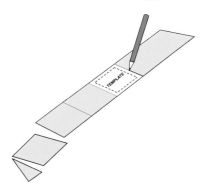

2 Hold the template firmly in place and draw around it with a sharp pencil or crayon, marking in the corner dots or seam lines. To save fabric, position patches close together or even touching. Don't worry if outlines positioned on the straight grain when drawn on striped fabrics do not always match the stripes when cut - this will add a degree of visual excitement to the patchwork!

3 Once you've drawn all the pieces needed, you are ready to cut the fabric, with either a rotary cutter and ruler, or a pair of sharp sewing scissors.

Basic hand and machine piecing

Patches can be joined together by hand or machine. Machine stitching is quicker, but hand assembly allows you to carry your patches around with you and work on them in every spare moment. The choice is yours. For techniques that are new to you, practise on scrap pieces of fabric until you feel confident.

Machine piecing

Follow the quilt instructions for the order in which to piece the individual patchwork blocks and then assemble the blocks together in rows.

1 Seam lines are not marked on the fabric, so stitch ¼in (6mm) seams using the machine needle plate, a ¼in (6mm) wide machine foot, or tape stuck to the machine as a guide. Pin two patches with right sides together, matching edges.

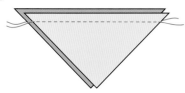

Set your machine at 10-12 stitches per inch (2.5cm) and stitch seams from edge to edge, removing pins as you feed the fabric through the machine.

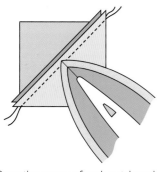

2 Press the seams of each patchwork block to one side before attempting to join it to another block.

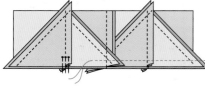

3 When joining rows of blocks, make sure that adjacent seam allowances are pressed in opposite directions to reduce bulk and make matching easier. Pin pieces together directly through the stitch line and to the right and left of the seam. Remove pins as you sew. Continue pressing seams to one side as you work.

Hand piecing

1 Pin two patches with right sides together, so that the marked seam lines are facing outwards.

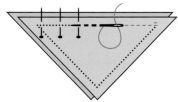

2 Using a single strand of strong thread, secure the corner of a seam line with a couple of back stitches.

3 Sew running stitches along the marked line, working 8-10 stitches per inch (2.5cm) and ending at the opposite seam line corner with a few back stitches. When hand piecing never stitch over the seam allowances.

4 Press the seams to one side, as shown in machine piecing (Step 2).

Inset seams.

In some patchwork layouts a patch will have to be sewn into an angled corner formed by the joining of two other patches. Use the following method whether you are machine or hand piecing. Don't be intimidated - this is not hard to do once you have learned a couple of techniques. The seam is sewn from the centre outwards in two halves to ensure that no tucks appear at the centre.

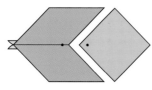

1 Mark with dots exactly where the inset will be joined and mark the seam lines on the wrong side of the fabric on the inset patch.

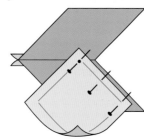

2 With right sides together and inset piece on top, pin through the dots to match the inset points. Pin the rest of the seam at right angles to the stitching line, along one edge of an adjoining patch.

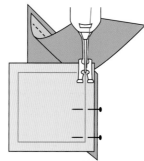

3 Stitch the patch in place along the seam line starting with the needle down through the inset point dots. Secure thread with a backstitch

if hand piecing, or stitch forward for a few stitches before backstitching, when machine piecing.

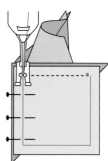

4 Pivot the patch, to enable it to align with the adjacent side of the angled corner, allowing you work on the second half of the seam. Starting with a pin at the inset point once again. Pin and stitch the second side in place, as before. Check seams and press carefully.

Hand appliqué

Good preparation is essential for speedy and accurate hand appliqué. The finger-pressing method is suitable for needle-turning application, used for simple shapes like leaves and flowers. Using a card template is the best method for bold simple motifs such as circles.

Finger-pressing:

1 To make your template, transfer the appliqué design on to stiff card using carbon paper, and cut out template. Trace around the outline of your appliquéd shape on to the right side of your fabric using a well sharpened pencil. Cut out shapes, adding a ¼in (6mm) seam allowance all around by eye.

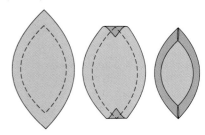

2 Hold shape right side up and fold under the seam, turning along your drawn line, pinch to form a crease. Dampening the fabric makes this very easy. When using shapes with 'points' such as leaves turn the seam allowance at the 'point' in first as shown in the diagram, then continue all round the shape. If your shapes have sharp curves you can snip the seam allowance to ease the curve. Take care not to stretch the appliqué shapes as you work.

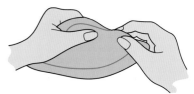

Card templates:

1 Cut out appliqué shapes as shown in step 1 of finger-pressing. Make a circular template from thin cardboard, without seam allowances.

2 Using a matching thread, work a row of running stitches close to the edge of the fabric circle. Place thin cardboard template in the centre of the fabric circle on the wrong side of the fabric.

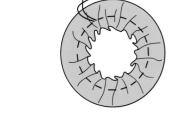

3 Carefully pull up the running stitches to gather up the edge of the fabric circle around the cardboard template. Press, so that no puckers or tucks appear on the right side. Then, carefully pop out the cardboard template without distorting the fabric shape.

Pressing stems:

For straight stems, place fabric face down and simply press over the 1/4in (6mm) seam allowance along each edge. You don't need to finish the ends of stems that are layered under other appliqué shapes. Where the end of the stem is visible simply tuck under the end and finish neatly.

Freezer paper:

1 Trace the appliqué shape onto the freezer paper and cut out. Make sure the coated side of the paper is next to the fabric and press onto the reverse. Cut out 1/4in (6mm) outside the paper edge. Baste the seam allowance to the reverse, snipping the seam allowance at curves and points will allow it to lay flat.

2 Using a matching thread, bring the needle up from the back of the block into the edge of the shape and proceed to blind–hem in place. This is a stitch where the motifs appear to be held on invisibly. Bring the thread out from

below through the folded edge of the motif, never on the top. Work around the complete shape, then turn the block over and remove the backing fabric from behind the appliqué shape leaving a 1/4in (6mm) seam allowance. Remove basting threads and peel off the freezer paper.

Needle-turning application

1 Take the appliqué shape and pin in position. Stroke the seam allowance under with the tip of the needle as far as the creased pencil line, and hold securely in place with your thumb. Using a matching thread, bring the needle up from the back of the block into the edge of the shape and proceed to blind-hem in place. This is a stitch where the motifs appear to be held on invisibly. Bring the thread out from below through the folded edge of the motif, never on the top. The stitches must be worked small, even and close together to prevent the seam allowance from unfolding and frayed edges appearing. Try to avoid pulling the stitches too tight, as this will cause the motifs to pucker up. Work around the whole shape, stroking under each small section before sewing.

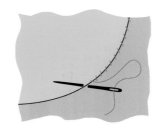

Quilting and finishing

When you have finished piecing your patchwork and added any borders, press it carefully. It is now ready for quilting.

Marking quilting designs and motifs

Many tools are available for marking quilting patterns, check the manufacturer's instructions for use and test on scraps of fabric from your project. Use an acrylic ruler for marking straight lines.

Stencils: Some designs require stencils, these can be made at home, by transferring the designs on to template plastic, or stiff cardboard. The design is then cut away in the form of long dashes, to act as guides for both internal and external lines. These stencils are a quick method for producing an identical set of repeated designs.

Preparing the backing and batting

• Remove the selvedges and piece together the backing fabric to form a backing at least 3in (7.5cm) larger all round than the patchwork top.

• For quilting choose a fairly thin batting, preferably pure cotton, to give your quilt a flat appearance. If your batting has been rolled up, unroll it and let it rest before cutting it to the same size as the backing.

• For a large quilt it may be necessary to join 2 pieces of batting to fit. Lay the pieces of batting on a flat surface so that they overlap by approx 8in (20cm). Cut a curved line through both layers.

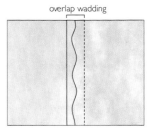

2. Carefully peel away the two narrow pieces and discard. Butt the curved cut edges back together. Stitch the two pieces together using a large herringbone stitch.

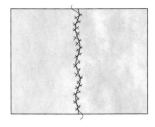

Basting the layers together

1 On a bare floor or large work surface, lay out the backing with wrong side uppermost. Use weights along the edges to keep it taut.

2 Lay the batting on the backing and smooth it out gently. Next lay the patchwork top, right side up, on top of the batting and smooth gently until there are no wrinkles. Pin at the corners and at the midpoints of each side, close to the edges.

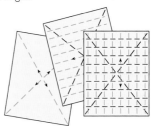

3 Beginning at the centre, baste diagonal lines outwards to the corners, making your stitches about 3in (7.5cm) long. Then, again starting at the centre, baste horizontal and vertical lines out to the edges. Continue basting until you have basted a grid of lines about 4in (10cm) apart over the entire quilt.

4 For speed, when machine quilting, some quilters prefer to baste their quilt sandwich layers together using rust proof safety pins, spaced at 4in (10cm) intervals over the entire quilt.

Hand quilting

This is best done with the quilt mounted on a quilting frame or hoop, but as long as you have basted the quilt well, a frame is not essential. With the quilt top facing upwards, begin at the centre of the quilt and make even running stitches following the design. It is more important to make even stitches on both sides of the quilt than to make small ones. Start and finish your stitching with back stitches and bury the ends of your threads in the batting.

Machine quilting

• For a flat looking quilt, always use a walking foot on your machine for straight lines, and a darning foot for free–motion quilting.

• It's best to start your quilting at the centre of the quilt and work out towards the borders, doing the straight quilting lines first (stitch–in –the–ditch) followed by the free–motion quilting.

• When free motion quilting stitch in a loose meandering style as shown in the diagrams. Do not stitch too closely as this will make the quilt feel stiff when finished. If you wish you can include floral themes or follow shapes on the printed fabrics for added interest.

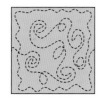

• Make it easier for yourself by handling the quilt properly. Roll up the excess quilt neatly to fit under your sewing machine arm, and use a table, or chair to help support the weight of the quilt that hangs down the other side.

Preparing to bind the edges

Once you have quilted or tied your quilt sandwich together, remove all the basting stitches. Then, baste around the outer edge of the quilt 1/4in (6mm) from the edge of the top patchwork layer. Trim the back and batting to the edge of the patchwork and straighten the edge of the patchwork if necessary.

Making the binding

1 Cut bias or straight grain strips the width required for your binding, making sure the grainline is running the correct way on your straight grain strips. Cut enough strips until you have the required length to go around the edge of your quilt.

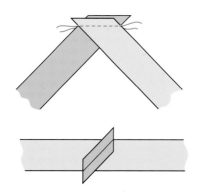

2 To join strips together, the two ends that are to be joined must be cut at a 45 degree angle, as above. Stitch right sides together, trim turnings and press seam open.

Binding the edges

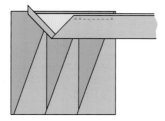

1 Cut starting end of binding strip at a 45-degree angle, fold a 1/4in (6mm) turning to wrong side along cut edge and press in place. With wrong sides together, fold strip in half lengthways, keeping raw edges level, and press.

2 Starting at the centre of one of the long edges, place the doubled binding on to the right side of the quilt keeping raw edges level. Stitch the binding in place starting 1/4in (6mm) in from the diagonal folded edge (see above). Reverse stitch to secure, and working 1/4in (6mm) in from edge of the quilt towards first corner of quilt. Stop 1/4in (6mm) in from corner and work a few reverse stitches.

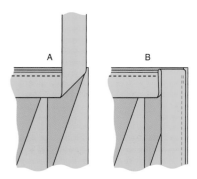

3 Fold the loose end of the binding up, making a 45-degree angle (see A). Keeping the diagonal fold in place, fold the binding back down, aligning the raw edges with the next side of the quilt. Starting at the point where the last stitch ended, stitch down the next side (see B).

4 Continue to stitch the binding in place around all the quilt edges in this way, tucking the finishing end

of the binding inside the diagonal starting section (see above).

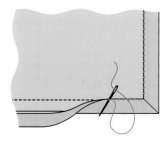

5 Turn the folded edge of the binding on to the back of the quilt. Hand stitch the folded edge in place just covering binding machine stitches, and folding a mitre at each corner.

Glossary of Terms

Appliqué The technique of stitching fabric shapes on to a background to create a design. It can be applied either by hand or machine with a decorative embroidery stitch, such as buttonhole, or satin stitch.

Backing The bottom layer of a quilt sandwich. It is made of fabric pieced to the size of the quilt top with the addition of about 3in (7.5cm) all around to allow for quilting take–up.

Basting or Tacking This is a means of holding two fabric layers or the layers of a quilt sandwich together temporarily with large hand stitches, or pins.

Batting or Wadding This is the middle layer, or padding in a quilt. It can be made of cotton, wool, silk or synthetic fibres.

Bias The diagonal grain of a fabric. This is the direction which has the most give or stretch, making it ideal for bindings, especially on curved edges.

Binding A narrow strip of fabric used to finish off the edges of quilts or projects; it can be cut on the straight grain of a fabric or on the bias.

Block A single design unit that when stitched together with other blocks create the quilt top. It is most often a square, hexagon, or rectangle, but it can be any shape. It can be pieced or plain.

Border A frame of fabric stitched to the outer edges of the quilt top. Borders can be narrow or wide, pieced or plain. As well as making the quilt larger, they unify the overall design and draw attention to the central area.

Chalk pencils Available in various colours, they are used for marking lines, or spots on fabric.

Cutting mat Designed for use with a rotary cutter, it is made from a special 'self–healing' material that keeps your cutting blade sharp. Cutting mats come in various sizes and are usually marked with a grid to help you line up the edges of fabric and cut out larger pieces.

Design Wall Used for laying out fabric patches before sewing. A large wall or folding board covered with flannel fabric or cotton batting in a neutral shade (dull beige or grey work well) will hold fabric in place so that an overall view can be taken of the placement.

Free–motion quilting Curved wavy quilting lines stitched in a random manner. Stitching diagrams are often given for you to follow as a loose guide.

Freezer Paper Paper which is plasticized on one side, usually sold on a roll. Originally used for wrapping meat for freezing it was found to adhere to fabric when pressed. It is useful for appliqué as it stays in place until peeled away without leaving any residue.

Fussy cutting This is when a template is placed on a particular motif, or stripe, to obtain interesting effects. This method is not as efficient as strip cutting, but yields very interesting results.

Grain The direction in which the threads run in a woven fabric. In a vertical direction it is called the lengthwise grain, which has very little stretch. The horizontal direction, or crosswise grain is slightly stretchy, but diagonally the fabric has a lot of stretch. This grain is called the bias. Wherever possible the grain of a fabric should run in the same direction on a quilt block and borders.

Inset seams or setting–in A patchwork technique whereby one patch (or block) is stitched into a 'V' shape formed by the joining of two other patches (or blocks).

Patch A small shaped piece of fabric used in the making of a patchwork pattern.

Patchwork The technique of stitching small pieces of fabric (patches) together to create a larger piece of fabric, usually forming a design.

Pieced quilt A quilt composed of patches.

Quilting Traditionally done by hand with running stitches, but for speed modern quilts are often stitched by machine. The stitches are sewn through the top, wadding and backing to hold the three layers together. Quilting stitches are usually worked in some form of design, but they can be random.

Quilting hoop Consists of two wooden circular or oval rings with a screw adjuster on the outer ring. It stabilises the quilt layers, helping to create an even tension.

Rotary cutter A sharp circular blade attached to a handle for quick, accurate cutting. It is a device that can be used to cut up to six layers of fabric at one time. It must be used in conjunction with a 'self–healing' cutting mat and a thick plastic ruler.

Rotary ruler A thick, clear plastic ruler printed with lines that are exactly ¼in (6mm) apart. Sometimes they also have diagonal lines printed on, indicating 45 and 60 degree angles. A rotary ruler is used as a guide when cutting out fabric pieces using a rotary cutter.

Sashing A piece or pieced sections of fabric interspaced between blocks.

Sashing Posts When blocks have sashing between them the corner squares are known as sashing posts.

Selvedges Also known as selvages, these are the firmly woven edges down each side of a fabric length. Selvedges should be trimmed off before cutting out your fabric, as they are more liable to shrink when the fabric is washed.

Stitch–in–the–ditch or Ditch quilting Also known as quilting–in–the–ditch. The quilting stitches are worked along the actual seam lines, to give a pieced quilt texture.

Template A pattern piece used as a guide for marking and cutting out fabric patches, or marking a quilting, or appliqué design. Usually made from plastic or strong card that can be reused many times.

Threads One hundred percent cotton or cotton–covered polyester is best for hand and machine piecing. Choose a colour that matches your fabric. When sewing different colours and patterns together, choose a medium to light neutral colour, such as grey or ecru. Specialist quilting threads are available for hand and machine quilting.

Walking foot or Quilting foot This is a sewing machine foot with dual feed control. It is very helpful when quilting, as the fabric layers are fed evenly from the top and below, reducing the risk of slippage and puckering.

Experience Ratings

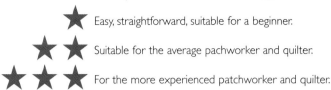

★ Easy, straightforward, suitable for a beginner.

★ ★ Suitable for the average pachworker and quilter.

★ ★ ★ For the more experienced patchworker and quilter.

Printed Fabrics

When ordering printed fabrics please note the following codes which precede the fabric number and two digit colour code.

AB is the code for the Amy Butler collection

GP is the code for the Kaffe Fassett collection

CM is the code for the Carla Miller collection

MN is the code for the Martha Negley collection

PJ is the code for the Philip Jacobs collection

The fabric collection can be viewed online at the following

www.westminsterfibers.com

Other ROWAN Titles Available

Patchwork and Quilting Book Number Four

A Colourful Journey

Kaffe Fassett's Caravan of Quilts

Kaffe Fassett's Quilt Road

Kaffe Fassett's Kaleidoscope of Quilts

Seven Easy Pieces

Rowan Living Book One

The Impatient Patchworker

The Impatient Embroiderer

All Drima and Sylko machine threads, Anchor embroidery threads, and Prym sewing aids, distributed in UK by Coats Crafts UK, P.O. Box 22, Lingfield House, Lingfield Point, McMullen Road, Darlington, Co. Durham, DL1 1YQ. Consumer helpline: 01325 394237.
Anchor embroidery thread and Coats sewing threads, distributed in the USA by Coats & Clark, 3430 Toringdon Way, Suite 301, Charlotte, NC 28277. Tel: 704 329 5800, Fax: 704 329 5821

R O W A N

Green Lane Mill, Holmfirth, West Yorkshire, England
Tel: +44 (0) 1484 681881   Fax: +44 (0) 1484 687920   Internet: www.knitrowan.com
Email: mail@knitrowan.com

Biographies

Pauline Smith

Pauline Smith has been a quilt maker and designer since a college visit to The American Museum in Bath in 1968. She makes most of Kaffe's quilts for the Rowan Patchwork And Quilting books, and as the Rowan patchwork co-ordinator, she works closely with everyone involved in producing the 'Patchwork and Quilting' series.

Betsy Menefee Rickles

Betsy began quilting in the late 90's. She found that piecing the quilt became the foundation of the project and that the free motion quilting, inspired by the movement in Kaffe's fabrics, made the design come alive. She likes using the solid shot cottons from Kaffe's collections as backing, not only do the quilting designs really pop but it's like quilting through butter. Betsy lives near Sisters, Oregon, and has worked for Jean and Valori Wells of the Stitchin' Post.

Roberta Horton

Roberta Horton of Berkeley, California has been a quiltmaker for over 30 years. She has taught and lectured worldwide. Her study and love of quilts has pushed her into developing many workshops and to the authoring of six books. Roberta was the recipient of the 2000 Silver Star Award presented by the International Quilt Association. This was in recognition of her lifetime body of work and the long-term effect it has had on quilting.

Rebekah Lynch

Fifteen years ago a patchwork class attracted Rebekah to Great Expectations quilt shop. Several lessons and many quilts later the student became the teacher. Introduced to a new world of color by Kaffe and Liza's book Glorious Patchwork, Rebekah has served as a 'stitcher' for their designs in later books. Her red Postcard quilt appears in *Kaffe Fassett's Quilt Road* and Katzahyden quilt featured in *Quiltmania* in 2006.

Brandon Mably

A regular contributor to the Rowan Patchwork books Brandon Mably has built a reputation as a quilt designer of simple, elegant quilts in restful colours. Brandon trained at The Kaffe Fassett Studio. He designs for the Rowan and Vogue Knitting magazine knitwear collections, and is the author of *Brilliant Knits* and *Knitting Color*.

Liza Prior Lucy

Liza Prior Lucy first began making quilts in 1990. She was so enthralled by the craftspeople she met and by the generously stocked quilt fabric shops in the States that quiltmaking soon became a passion. Liza originally trained as a knitwear designer and produced features for needlework magazines. She also owned and operated her own needlepoint shop in Washington, D.C. Liza met Kaffe when she was working as a sales representative for Rowan Yarns. They worked closely together to write and produce the quilts for the books *Glorious Patchwork*, *Passionate Patchwork* and *Kaffe Fassett's V&A Quilts*.

Mary Mashuta

California quiltmaker Mary Mashuta has been making quilts and wearables for over thirty years. She is a professionally trained teacher who has been teaching internationally since 1985. Her classes always stress easily understood colour and design. She knows that no quilter can own too much fabric, and she enjoys discovering new blocks to showcase personal collections. Mary has authored five books and numerous magazine articles.

Distributors and Stockists

Overseas Distributors of Rowan Fabrics

AUSTRALIA
XLN Fabrics
2/21 Binney Road,
Kings Park
New South Wales 2148
Tel: 61 2 96213066

AUSTRIA
Rhinetex bv
Geurdeland 7 (de Schalm)
6673 DR Andelst
P.O. Box 204
The Netherlands
Tel: +31 488 48 00 30
Fax: +31 488 48 04 22
www.rhinetex.com

BELGIUM
Rhinetex bv
Geurdeland 7 (de Schalm)
6673 DR Andelst
P.O. Box 204
The Netherlands
Tel: +31 488 48 00 30
Fax: +31 488 48 04 22
www.rhinetex.com

BRAZIL
Coats Corrente
Rua Do Manifesto, 705
Ipirangu
Sao Paulo
Brazil 04209

CANADA
Telio
625 Rue DesLauriers
Montreal, QC,
Tel: 514 271 4607
Fax: 514 271 7734
Email: info@telio.com

CZECH REPUBLIC
Coats Czecho s.r.o.
Staré Mesto 246, 569 32
Tel: 00420 461 616633
Fax: 00420 461 542544
www.coatscrafts.cz

DENMARK
Coats HP A/S
Nannasgade 28
2200 Köpenhamn
Tel: + 45 35 83 50 20
Fax: + 45 35 82 15 10
www.hpgruppen.dk

FINLAND
Coats Opti Oy
Ketjutie 3, 04220 Kerava
Tel: +358 9 274 871
Fax: +358 9 242 6186
www.coatscrafts.fi

FRANCE
Rhinetex bv
Geurdeland 7 (de Schalm)
6673 DR Andelst
P.O. Box 204
The Netherlands
Tel: +31 488 48 00 30
Fax: +31 488 48 04 22
www.rhinetex.com

GERMANY
Rhinetex bv
Geurdeland 7 (de Schalm)
6673 DR Andelst
P.O. Box 204
The Netherlands
Tel: +31 488 48 00 30
Fax: +31 488 48 04 22
www.rhinetex.com

HOLLAND
Rhinetex bv
Geurdeland 7 (de Schalm)
6673 DR Andelst
P.O. Box 204
The Netherlands
Tel: +31 488 48 00 30
Fax: +31 488 48 04 22
www.rhinetex.com

ICELAND
Storkurinn
Kjorgardi
Laugavegi 59
Reykjavik
Tel: (354) 551 82 58

IRELAND
Rowan Yarns
Green Lane Mill
Holmfirth HD9 2DX
Tel: 0044 (0) 1484 681881
Fax: 0044 (0) 1484 687920
www.knitrowan.com

ITALY
Coats Cucirini S.r.L
Via Vespucci 2, 20124 Milano
Tel: 02-63615224-234-235
Fax: 02-6596509
www.coatscucirini.it

JAPAN
Yokota & Co Ltd
5-14 2 Chome
Minamikyuhoojimachi
Chuo-Ku
Osaka
Tel: 81 6 6251 7179

LUXEMBURG
Rhinetex bv
Geurdeland 7 (de Schalm)
6673 DR Andelst
P.O. Box 204
The Netherlands
Tel: +31 488 48 00 30
Fax: +31 488 48 04 22
www.rhinetex.com

NEW ZEALAND
Fabco Limited
PO Box 84-002
Westgate
Auckland 1250
Tel: 64 9 411 9996
Fax: 64 9 411 9506
Email: info@fabco.co.nz

NORWAY
Coats Knappehuset
AS Pb. 100 Ulset, 5873 Bergen
Tel: + 47 555339300
Fax: + 47 55539393
www.coatscrafts.no

POLAND
Coats Polska Sp.z o.o.
ul.Kaczencowa 16, 91-214 Lódz
Tel: (48) (42) 254 0400
Fax: (48) (42) 254 0422
www.coatscrafts.pl

PORTUGAL
Coats & Clark
Quinta de Cravel, Apartado 444,
4431-968 V.N. Gaia
Tel: (00351) 223770700
Fax: (00351) 223770157
www.coatscrafts.com.pt

RUSSIA
Coats LLC
140060 Moscow Reg. Luberetsky
District
Oktiabrsky, Lelina Str. 53A
Tel: +74955105184
Fax: +74955105184
www.coatscrafts.ru

SLOVAKIA
Coats s.r.o. Kopcianska 94
851 01 Bratislava
Tel: 00421 2 63532314
www.coatscrafts.sk

SOUTH AFRICA
Arthur Bales PTY Ltd
PO Box 44644
Linden 2104
Tel: 27 11 888 2401
Fax: 27 11 782 6137
Email: arthurb@new.co.za

SOUTH KOREA
Coats Korea Co Ltd,
5F Kuckdong B/D, 935-40
Bangbae- Dong,
Seocho-Gu, Seoul.
Tel: (82) 2 521 6262
Fax: (82) 2 521 5181

SPAIN
Coats Fabra
Sant Adrià, 20, 08030 Barcelona
Tel: 0034 9302908400
www.coatscrafts.es

SWEDEN
Coats Expotex AB
Stationsvägen 2, 516 31 Dalsjöfors
Tel: 46 33 720 900
Fax: 46 31 471 650
www.coatscrafts.se

SWITZERLAND
Rhinetex bv
Geurdeland 7 (de Schalm)
6673 DR Andelst
P.O. Box 204
The Netherlands
Tel: +31 488 48 00 30
Fax: +31 488 48 04 22
www.rhinetex.com

TAIWAN
Long Teh Trading Co
6F #156, Shifu Road
Taichung City
Tel: 886 4 2225 6698
Fax: 886 4 2225 6697

TURKEY
Coats Turkiye, Kavacık Mah. Ekinciler
Cad. Necip Fazıl Sok. No:8 Kat:5
34810 Beykoz Istanbul
Tel: +90 216 425 88 10
Fax: +90 216 425 66 99
www.coatsturkiye.com.tr

UK
Rowan Yarns
Green Lane Mill
Holmfirth HD9 2DX
Tel: 0044 (0) 1484 681881
Fax: 0044 (0) 1484 687920
www.knitrowan.com

USA
Westminster Fibers
3430 Toringdon Way
Suite 301,
Charlotte,
NC 28277
Tel: 704-329-5822
Email: fabric@westminsterfibers.com
Internet: westminsterfibers.com